DELIGHTFUL DOGS

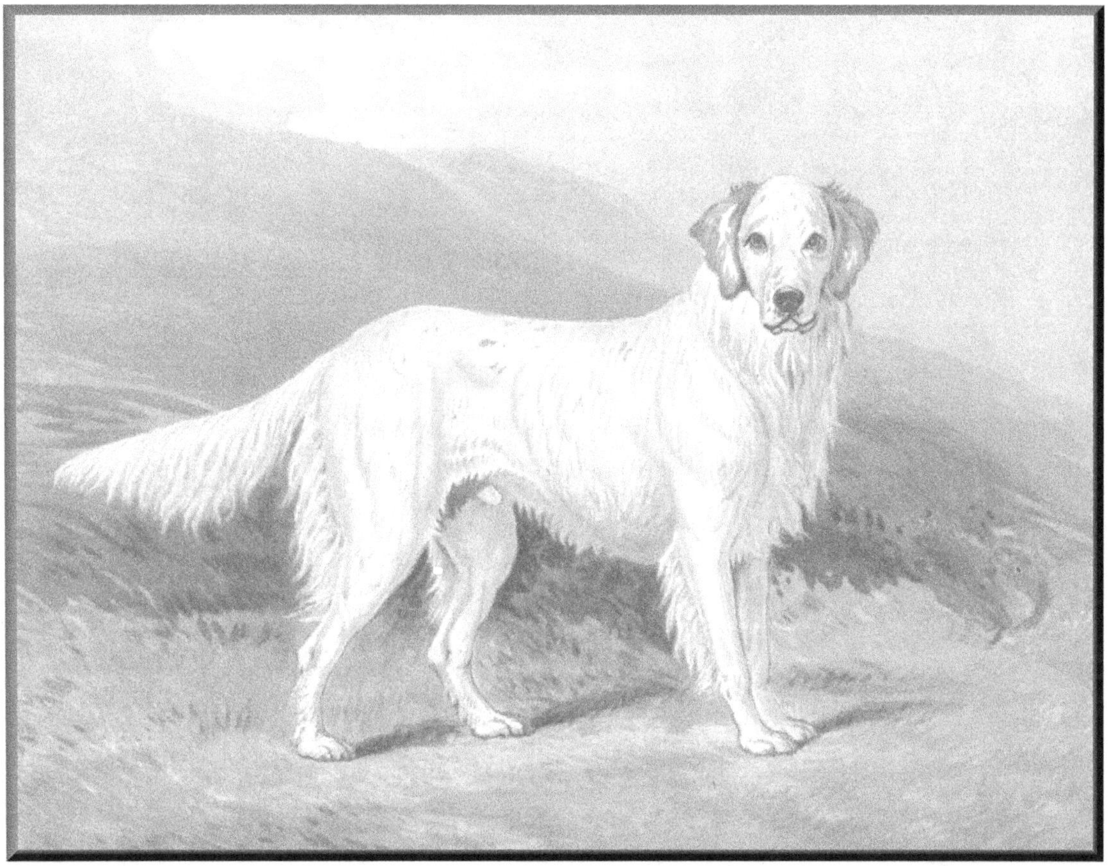

GRAYSCALE ADULT COLORING BOOK

OLDE GLORIE STUDIOS

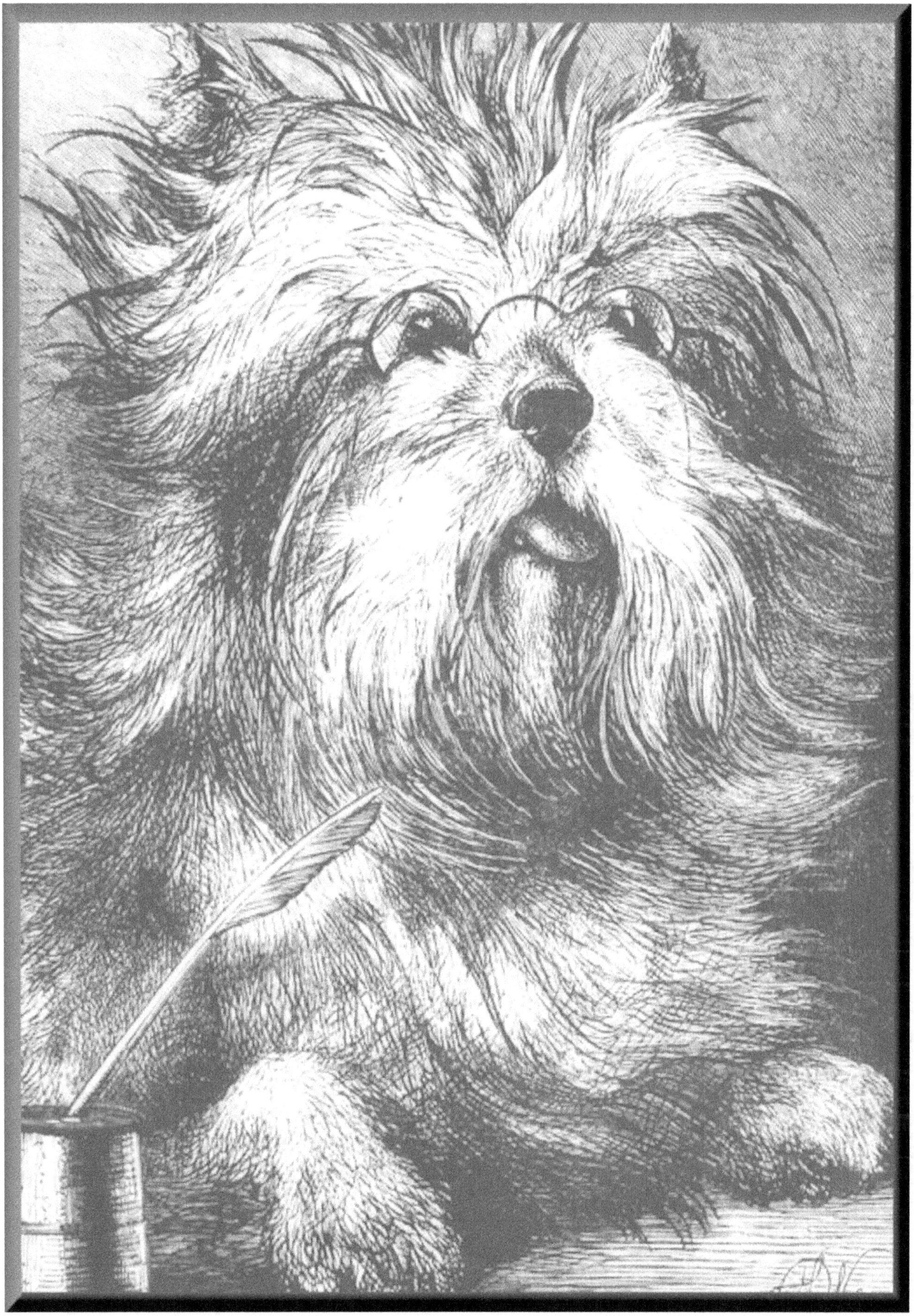

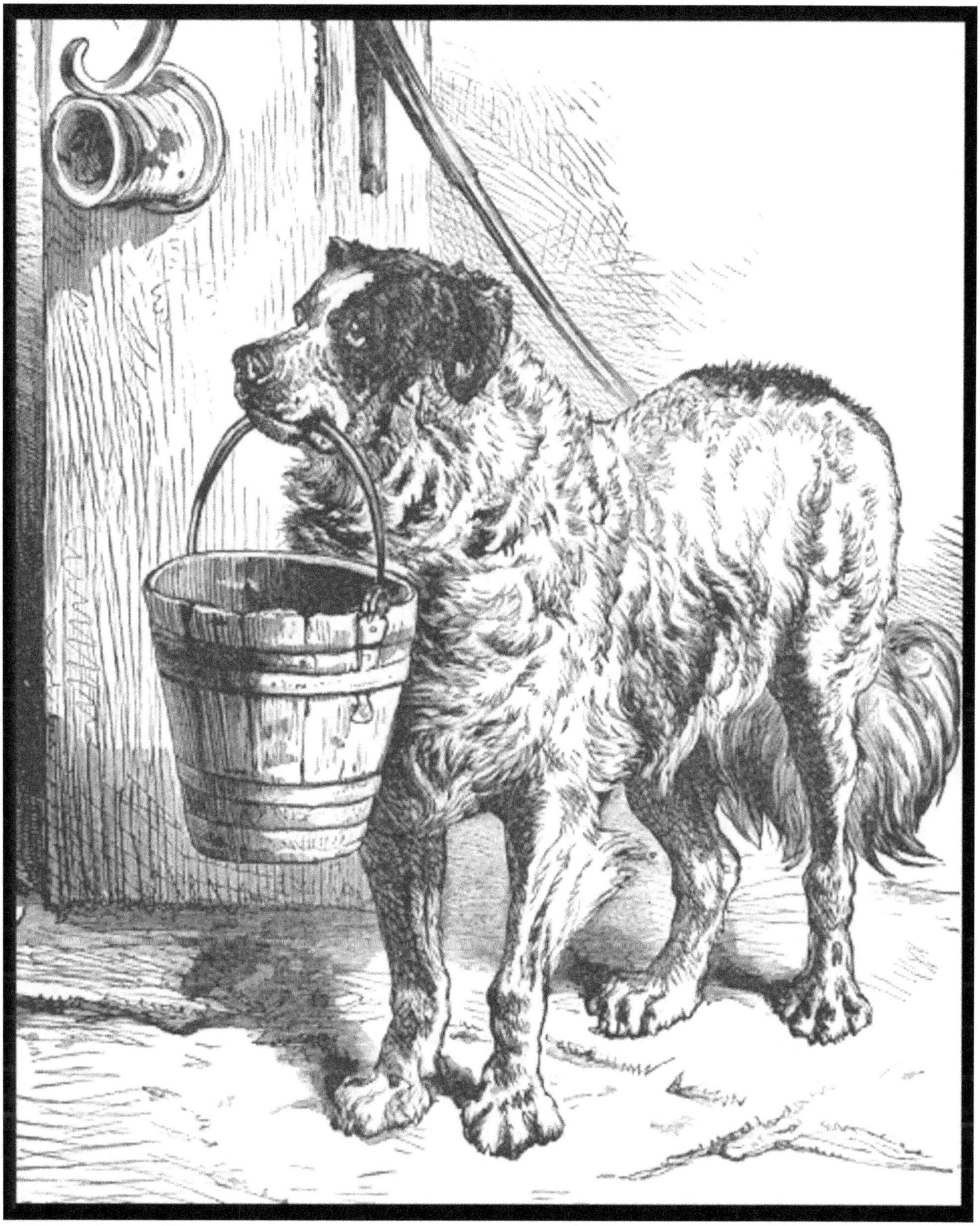

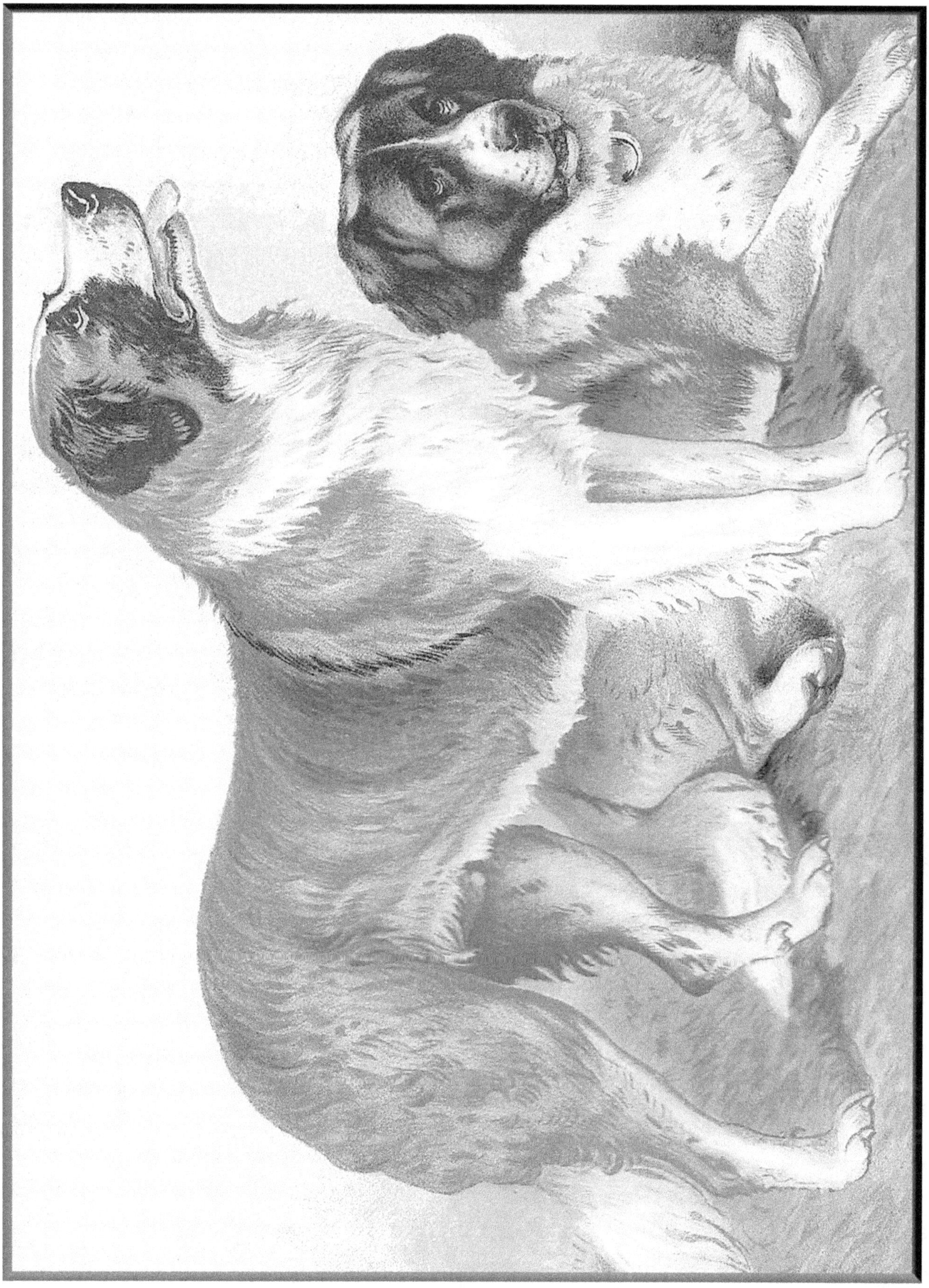

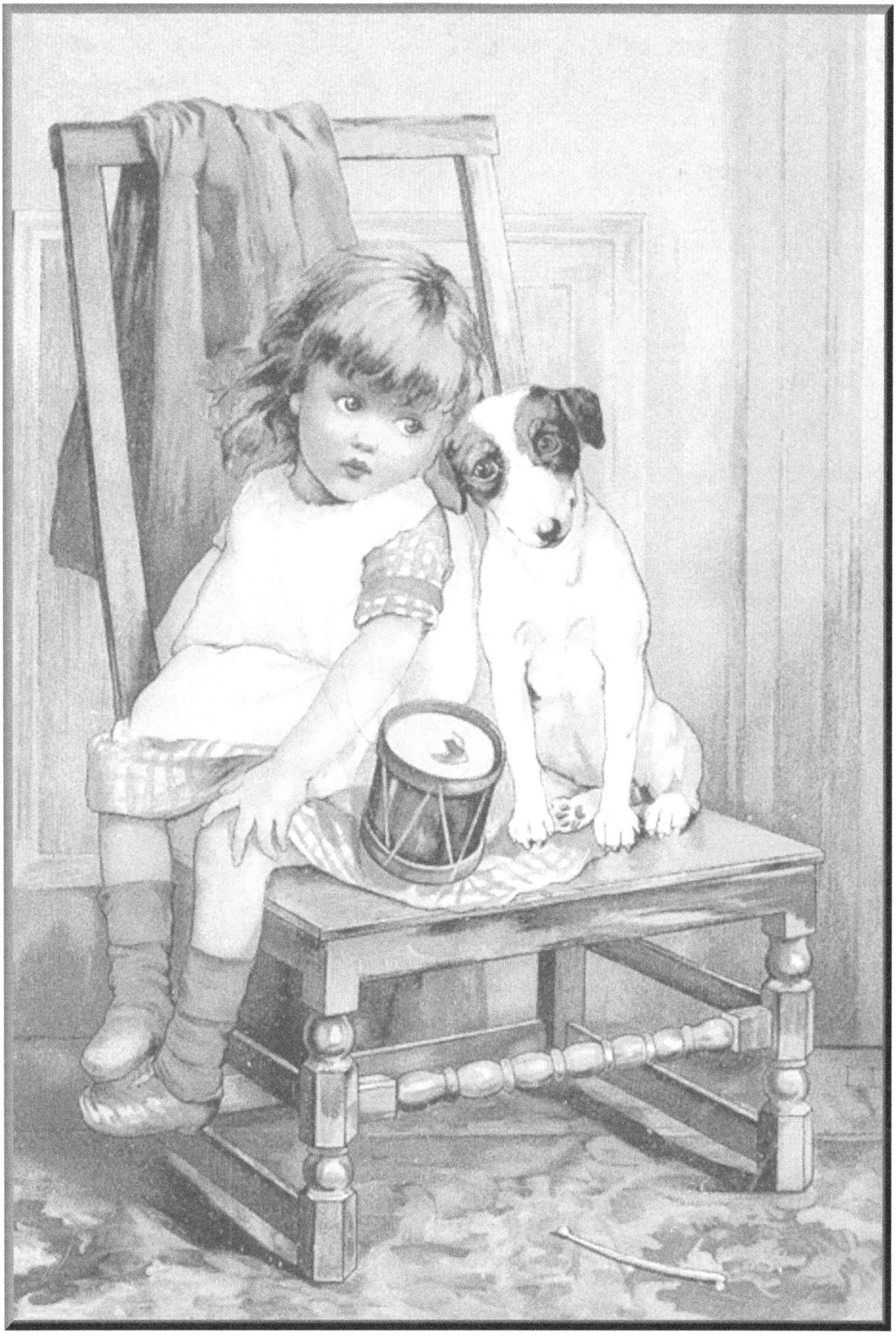

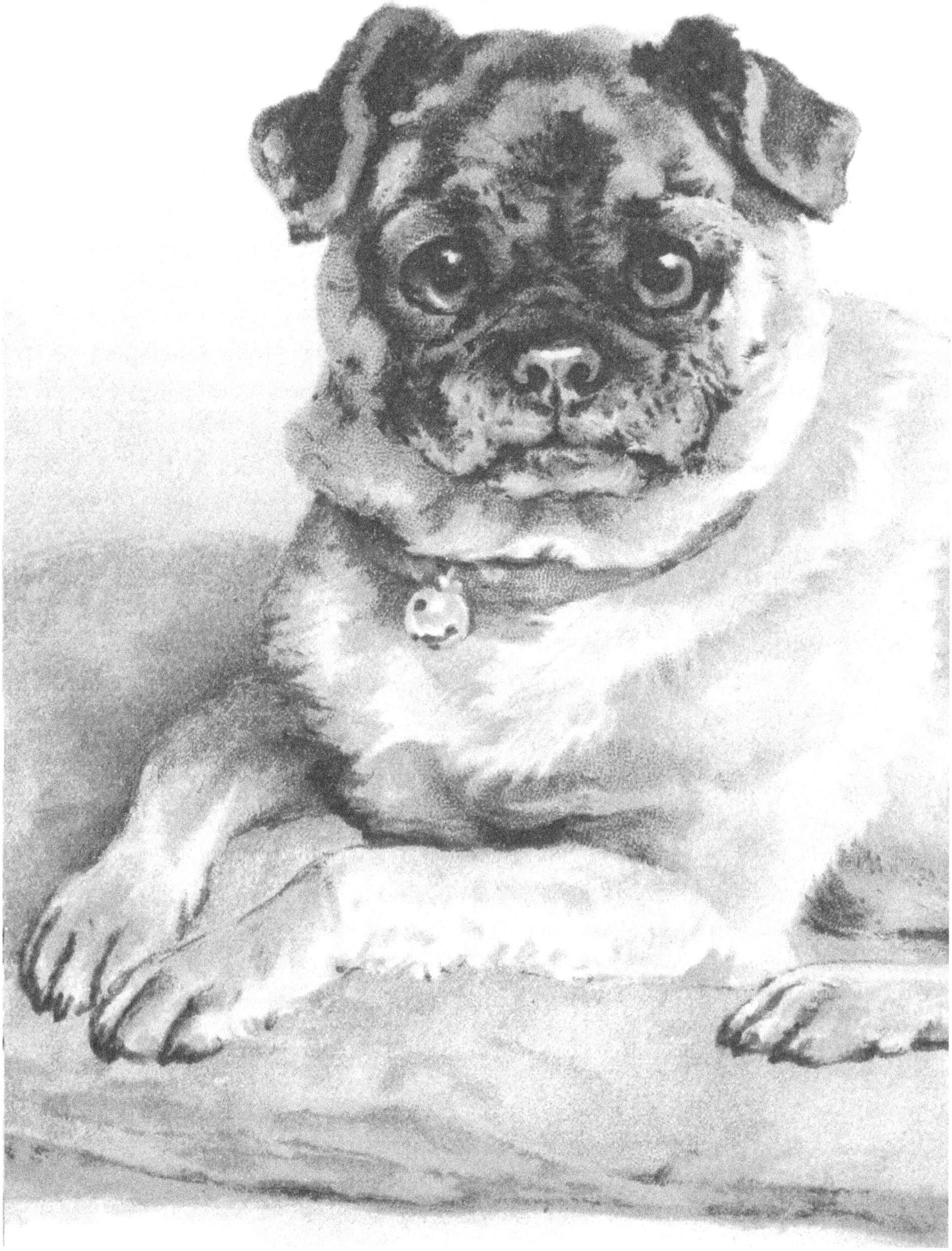

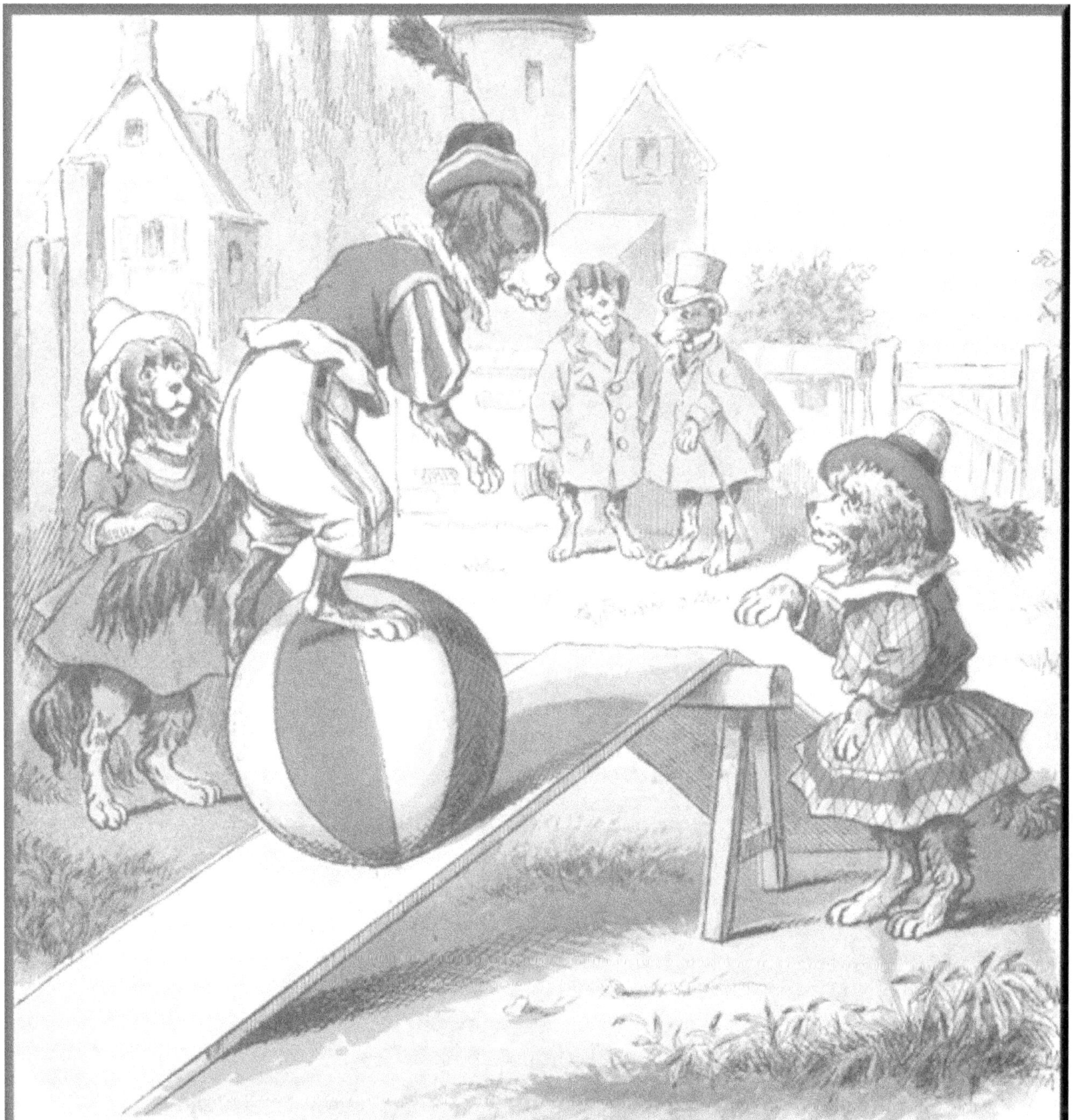

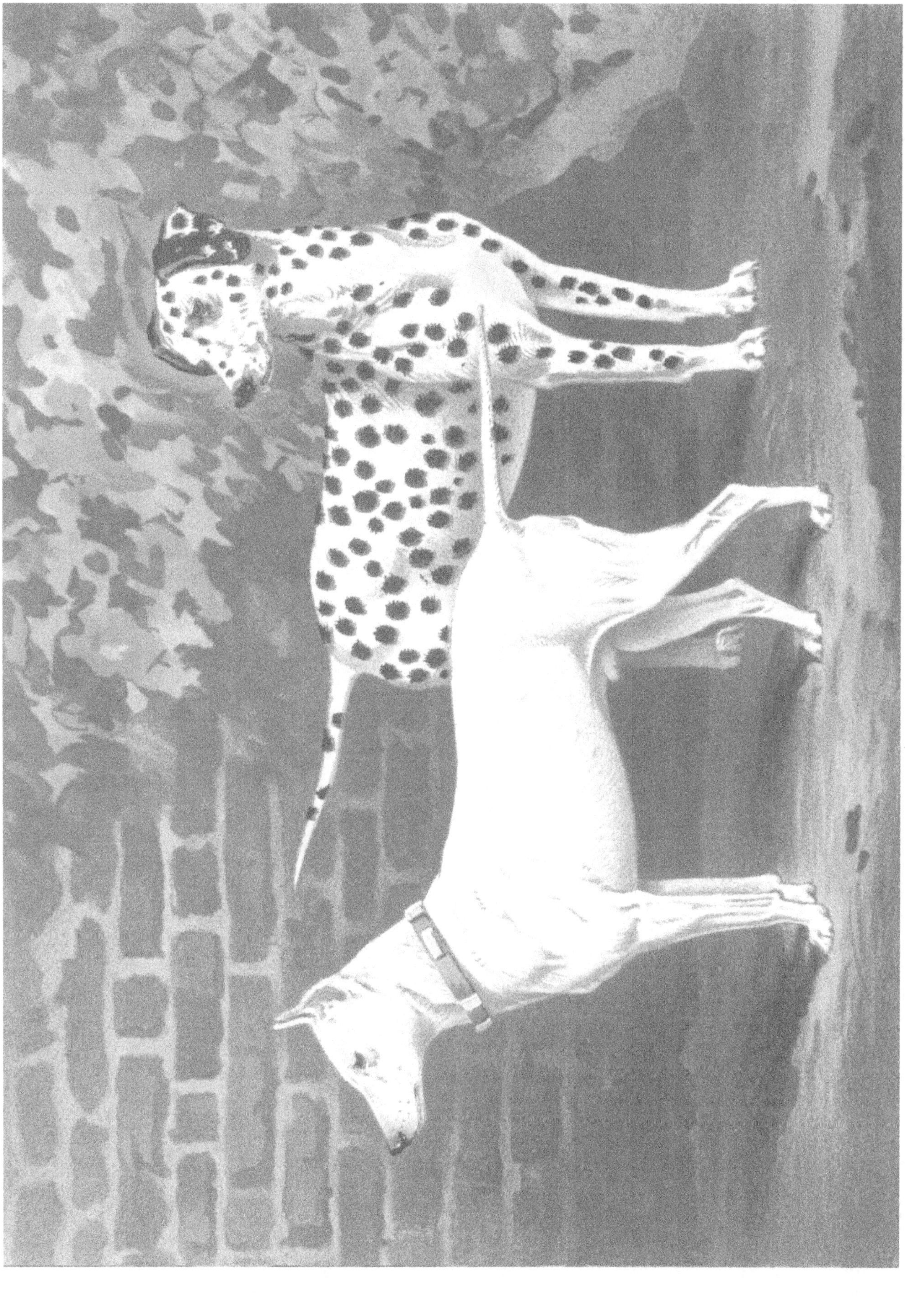

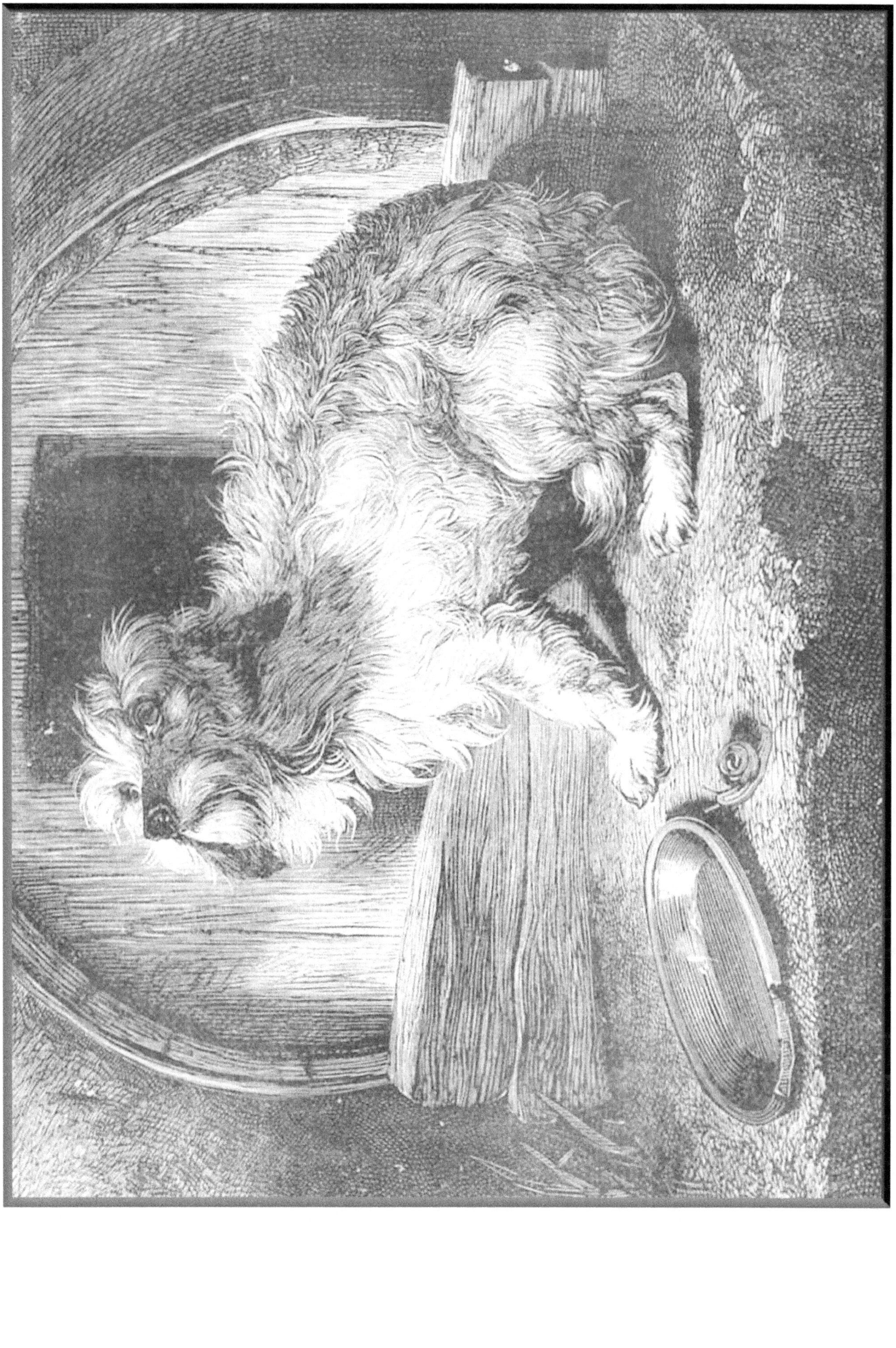

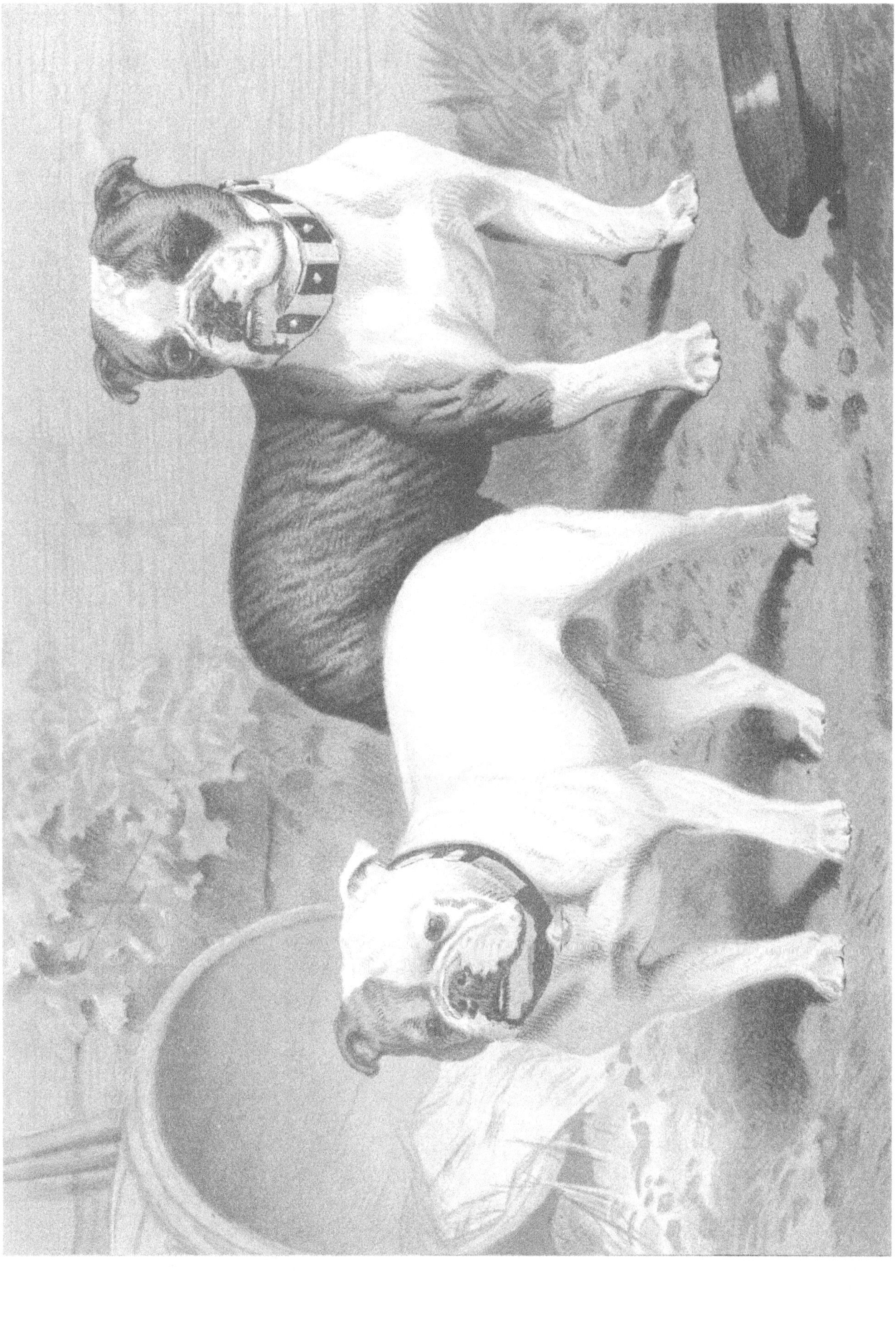

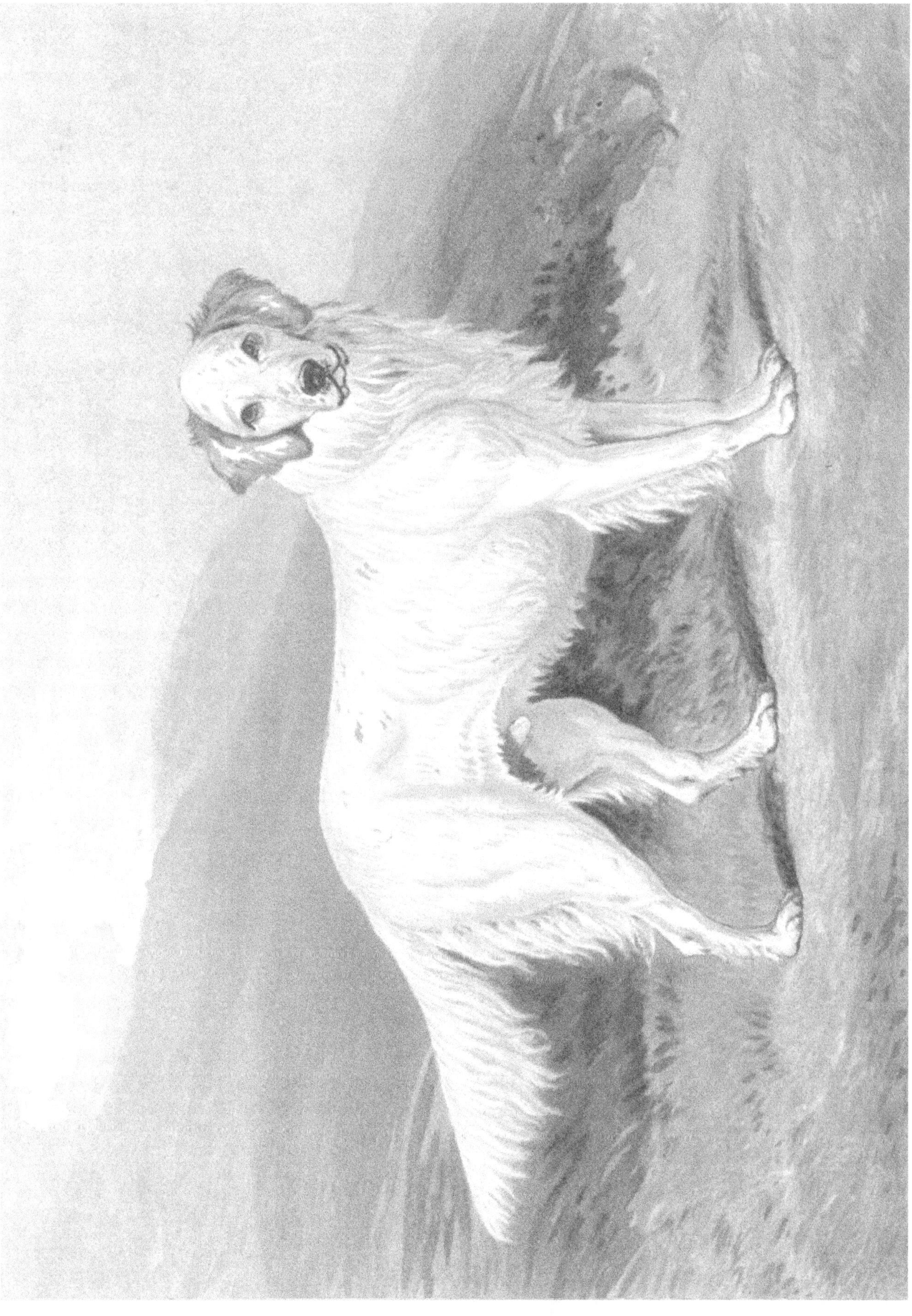

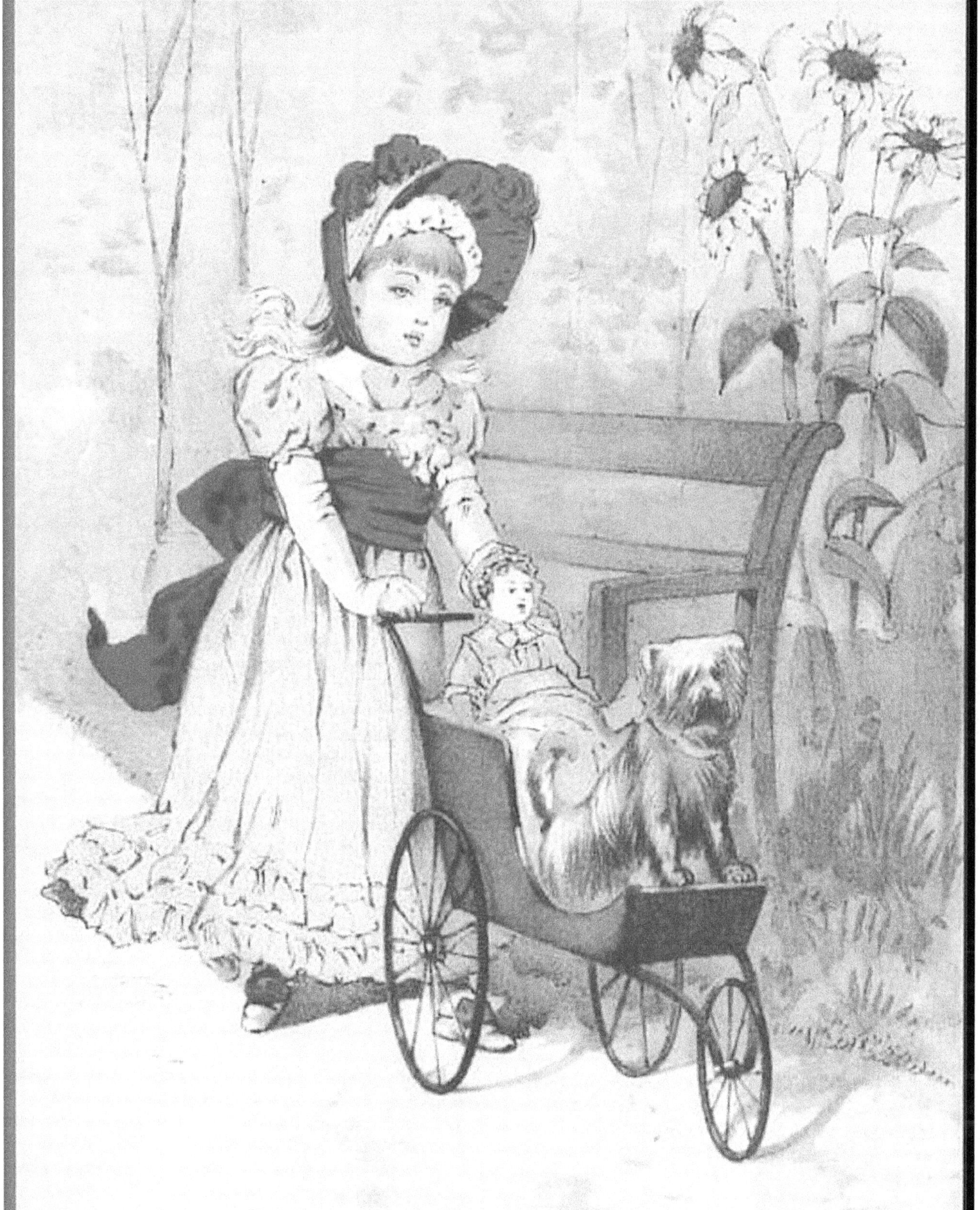

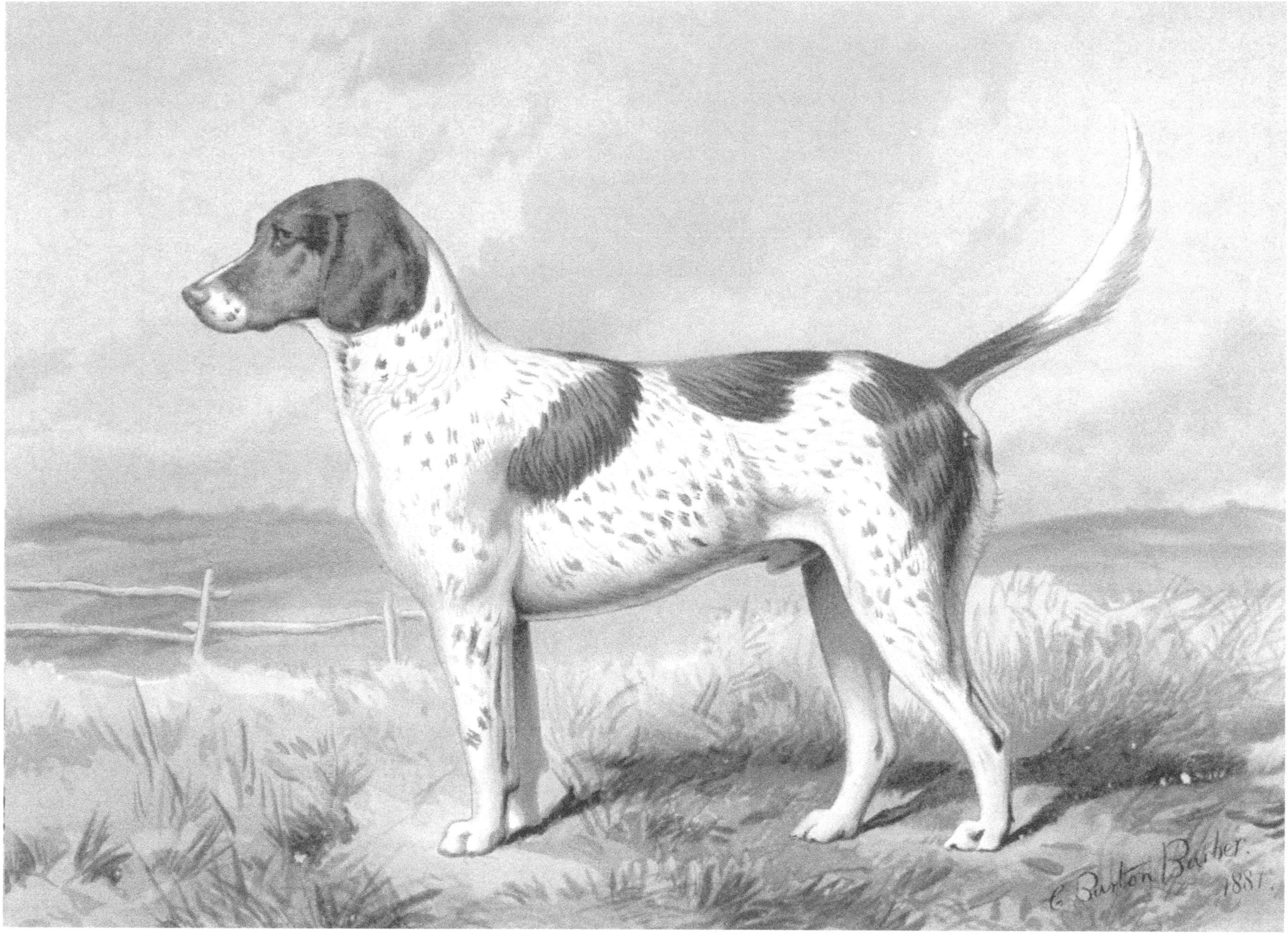
C. Burton Barber.
1881.

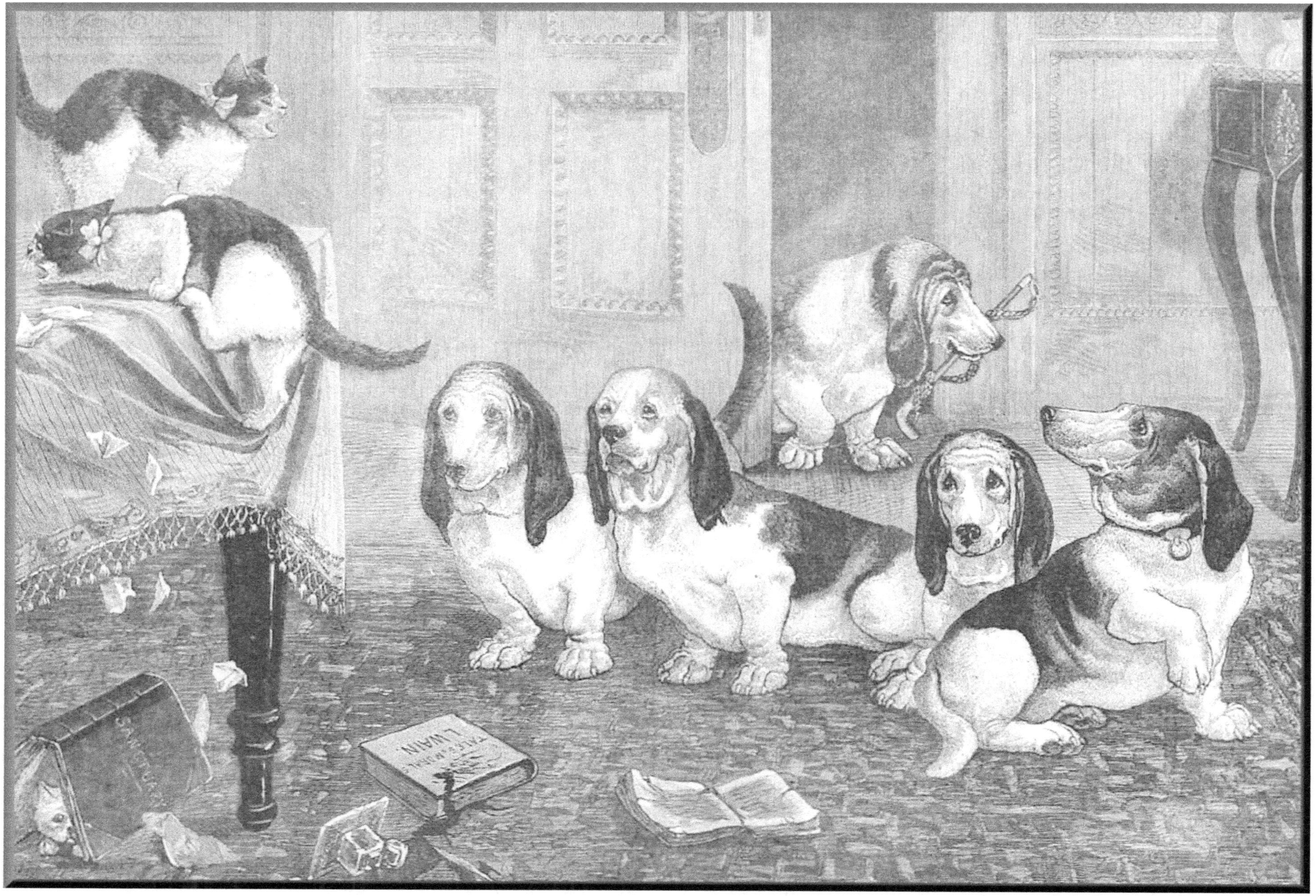
L. WAIN

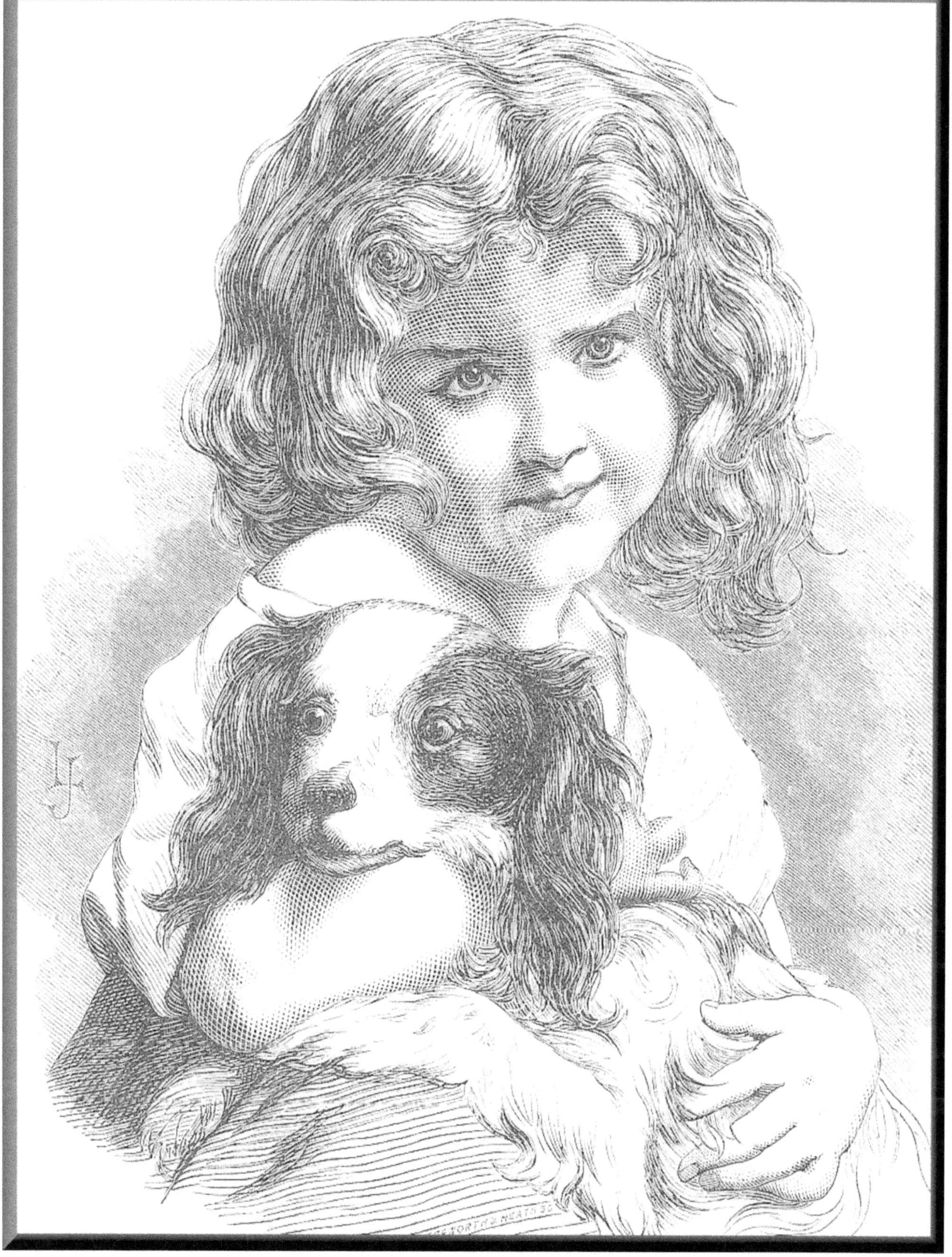

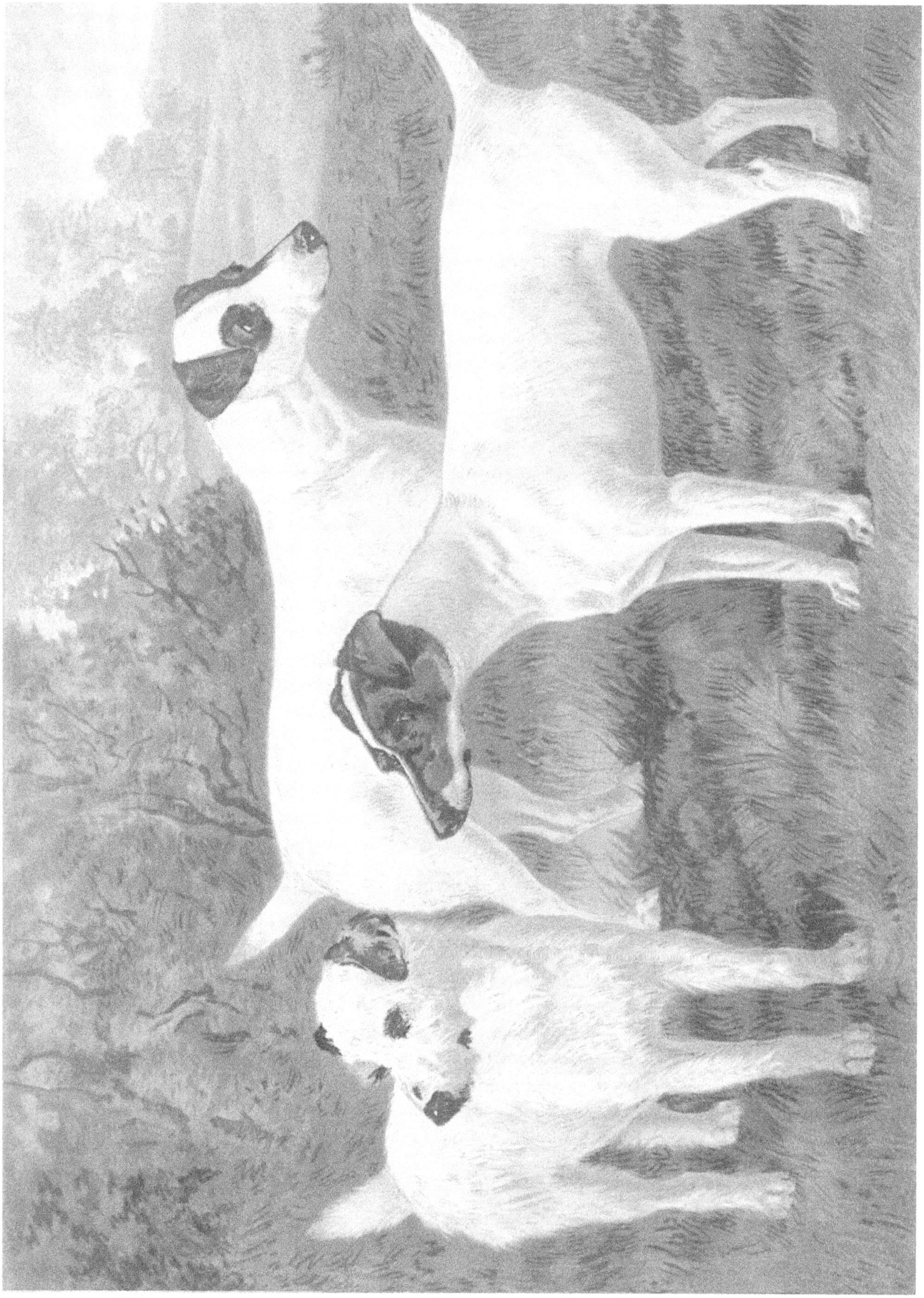

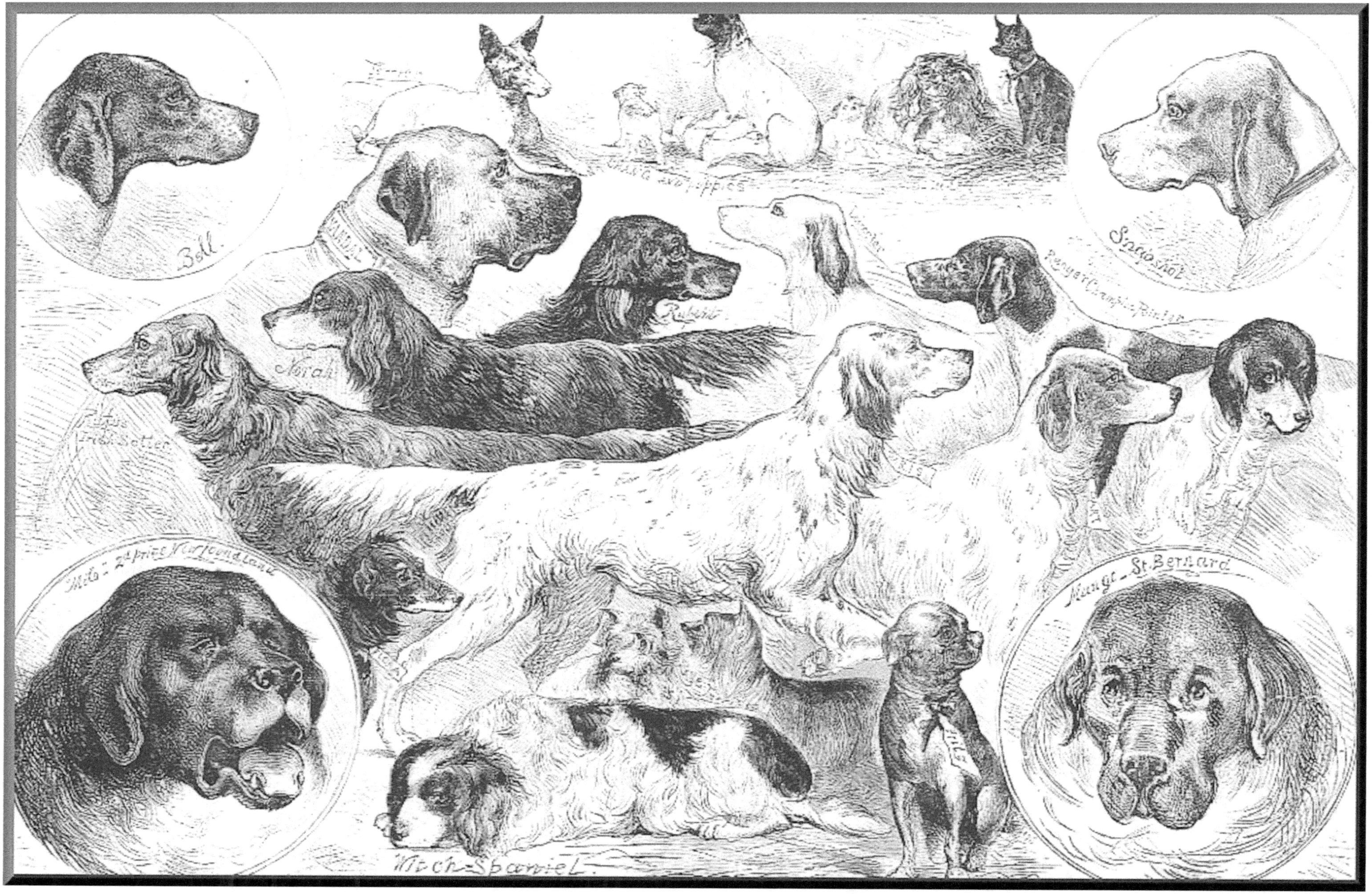
Bell.
Norah
Rupert
Snapshot
Mange - St Bernard
Witch - Spaniel.

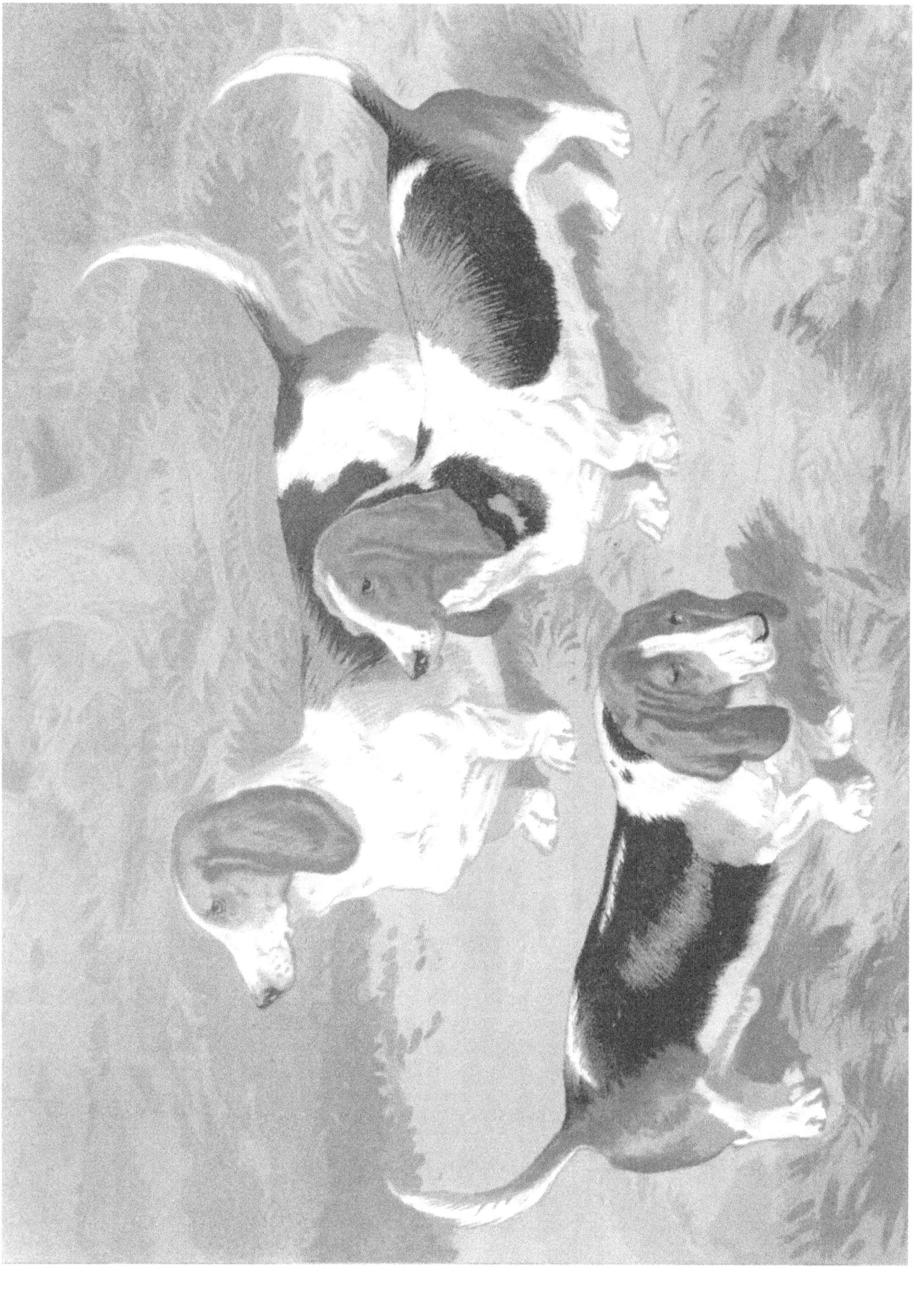

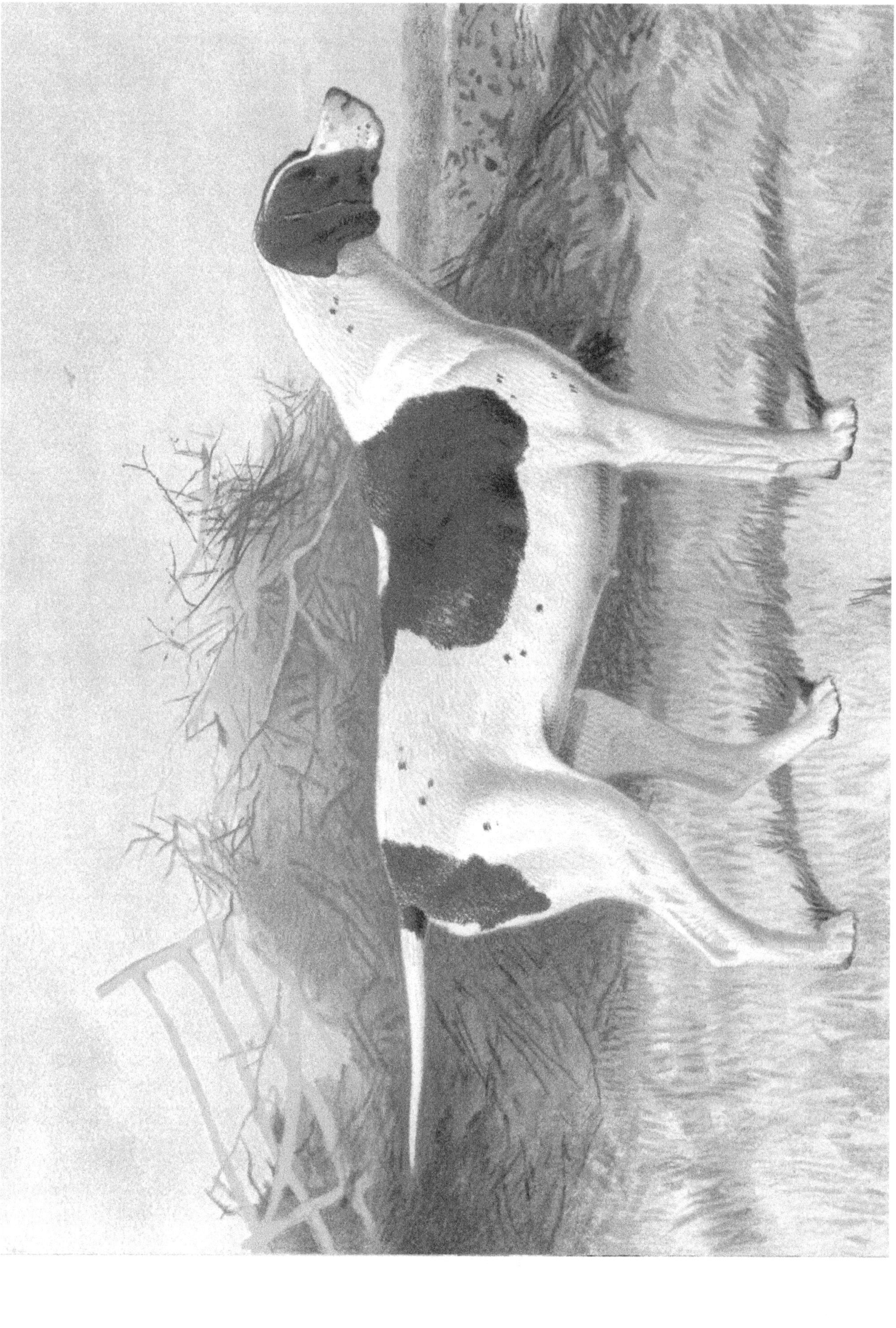

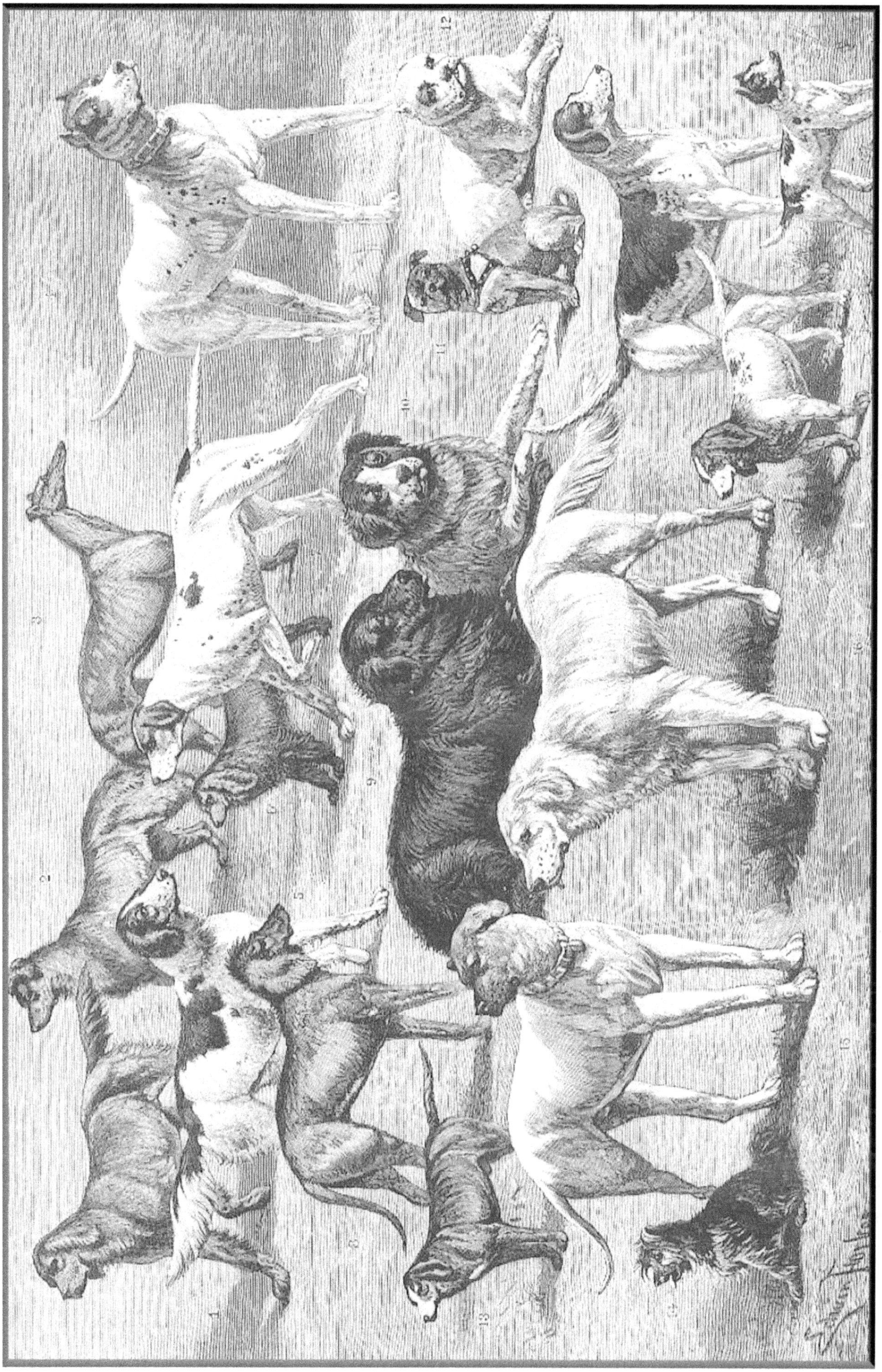

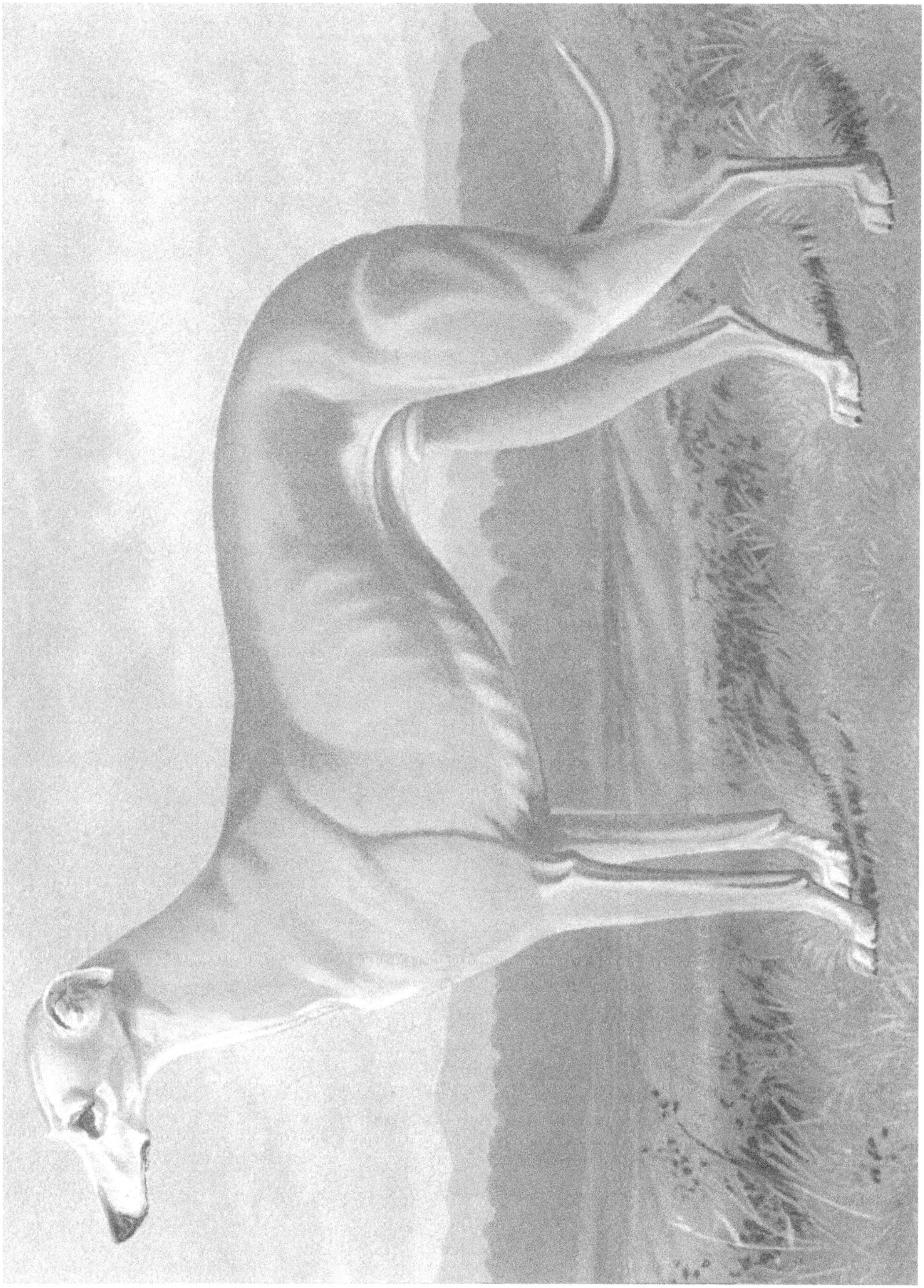

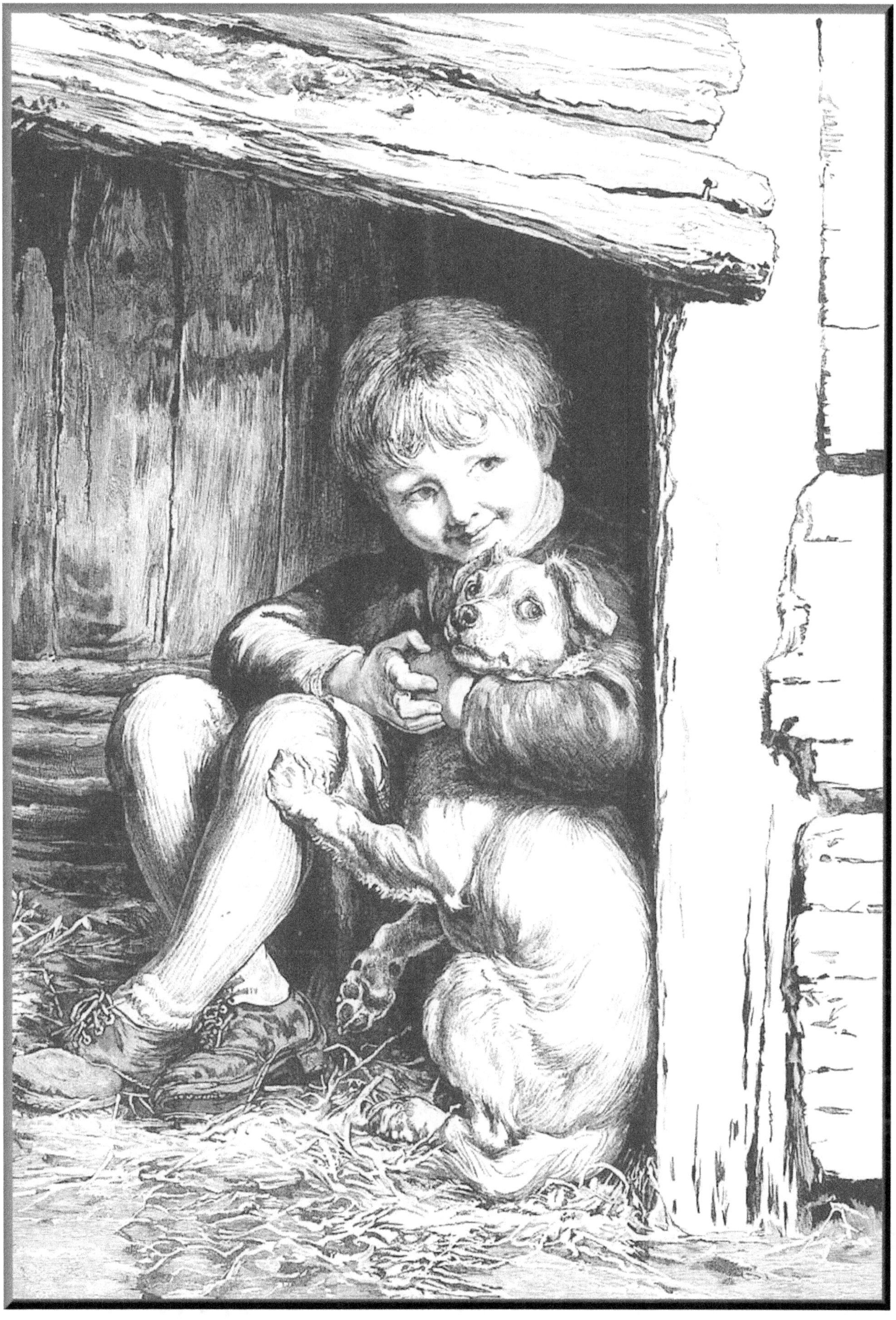

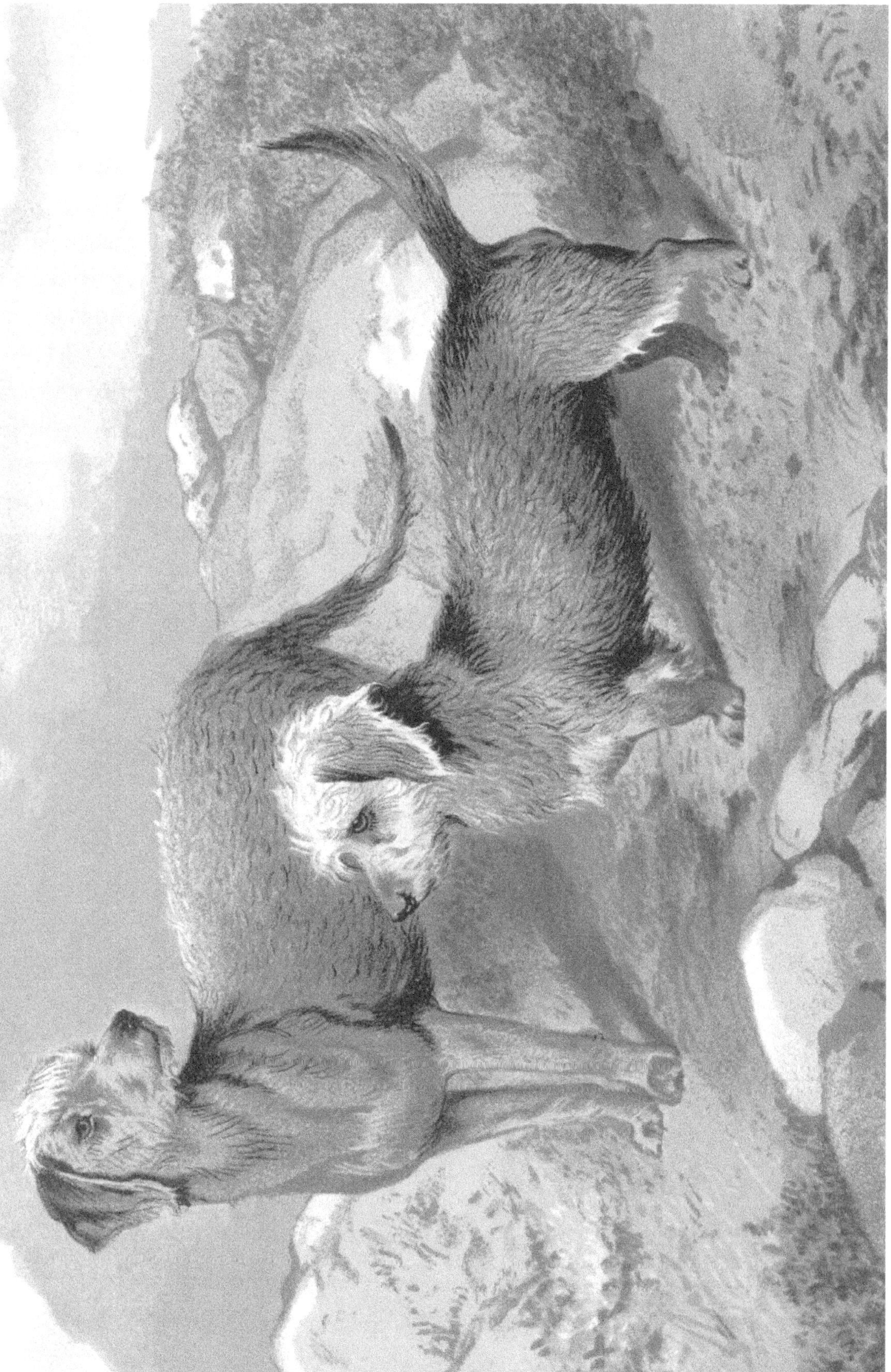

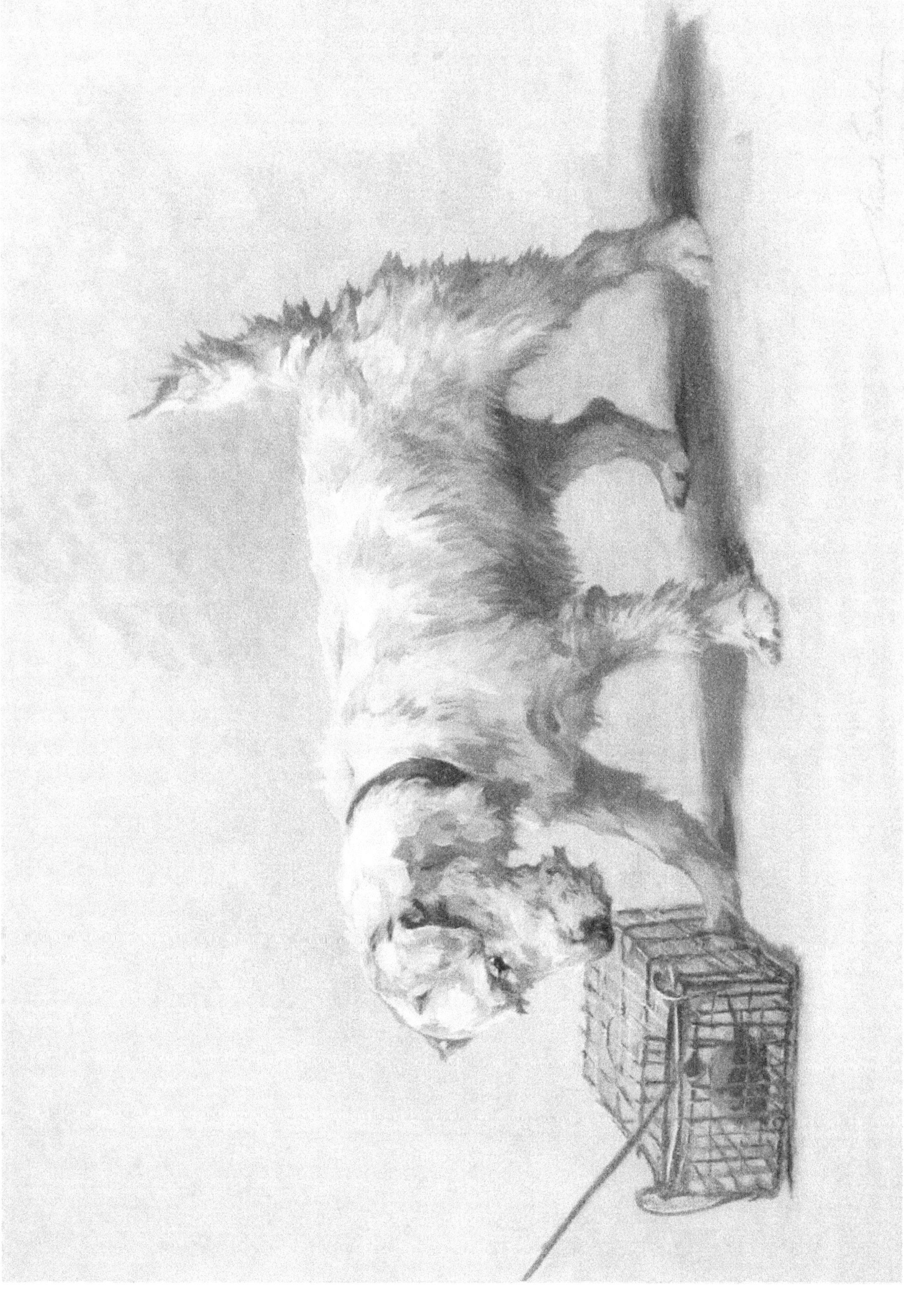

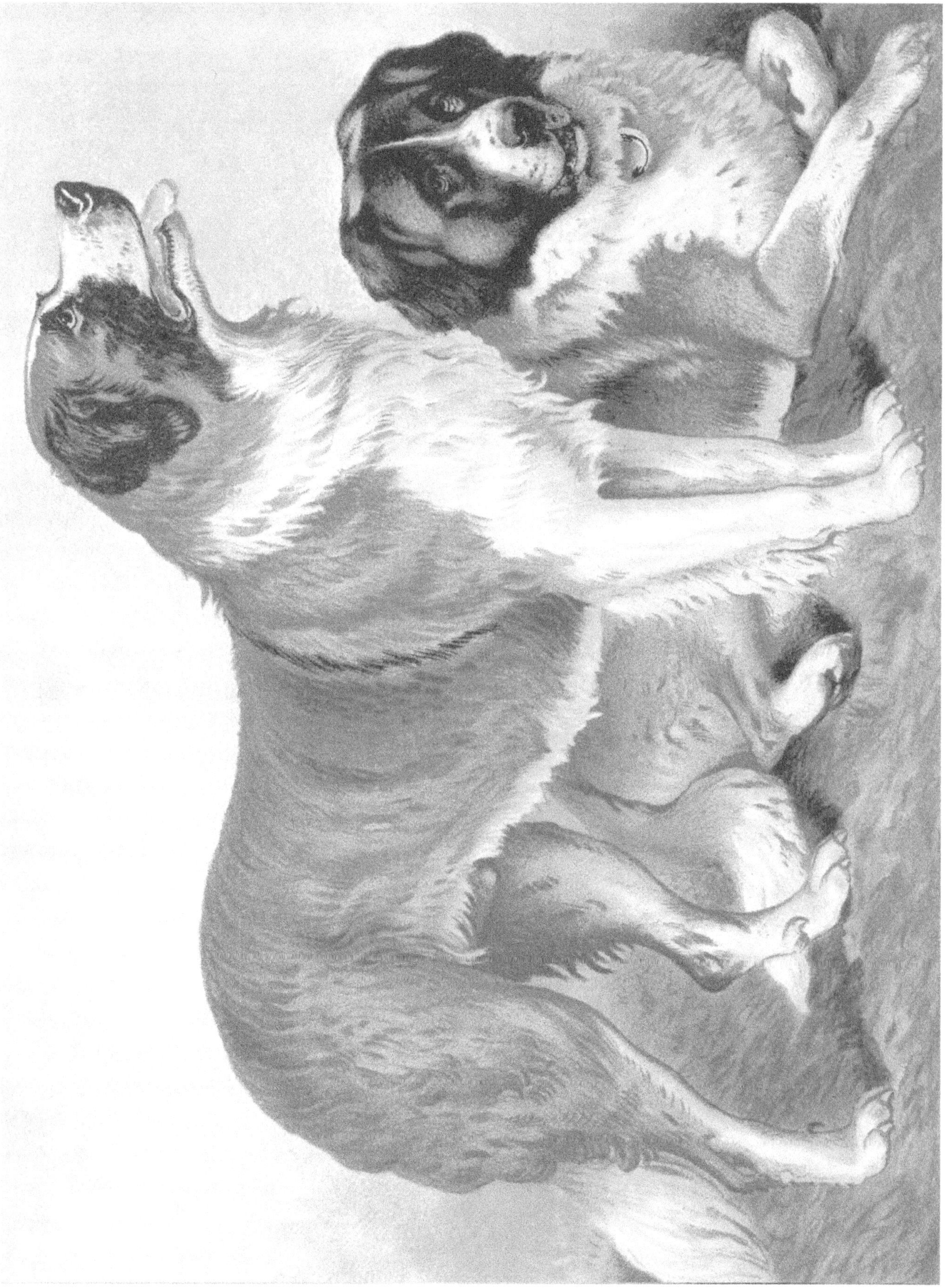

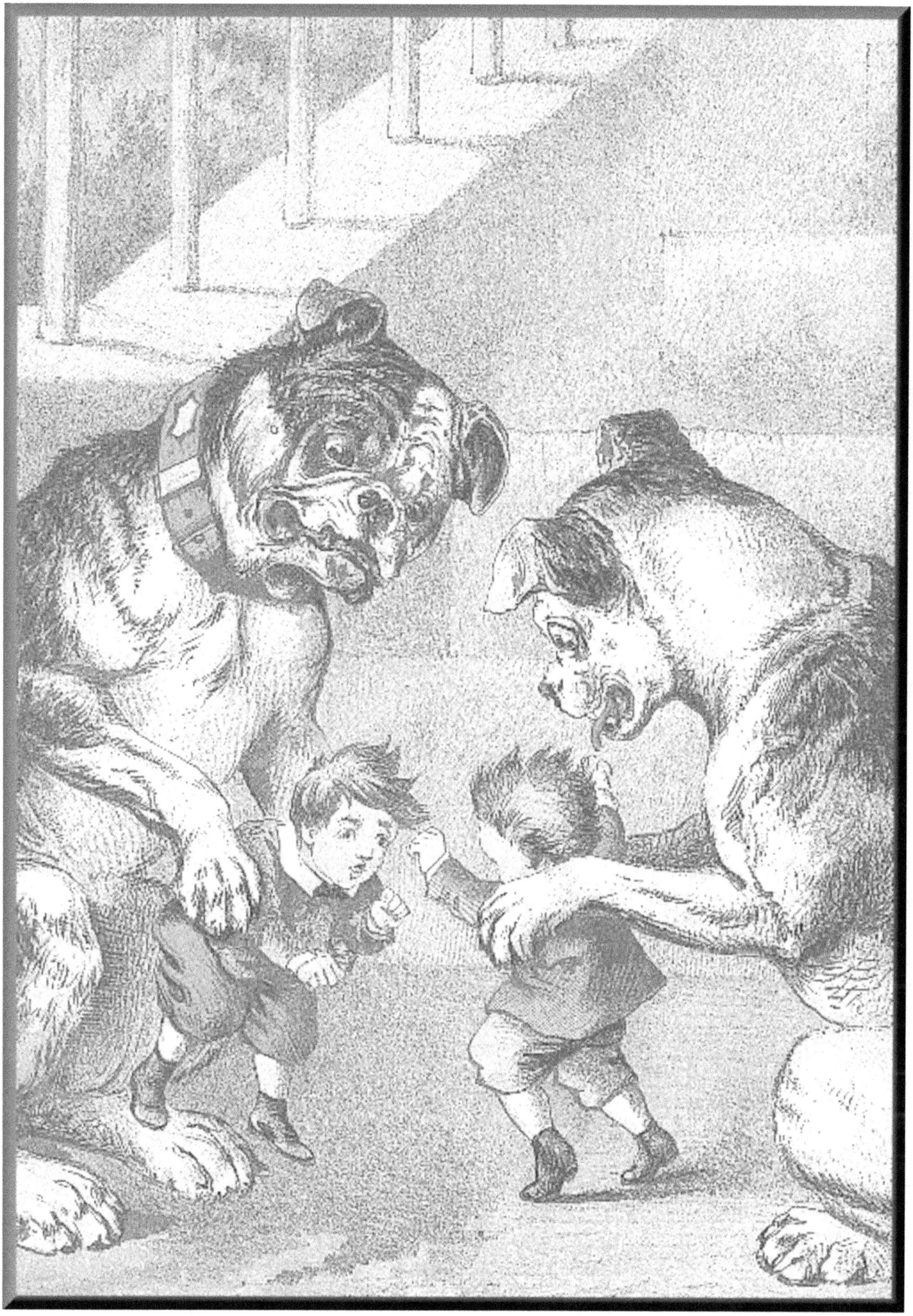

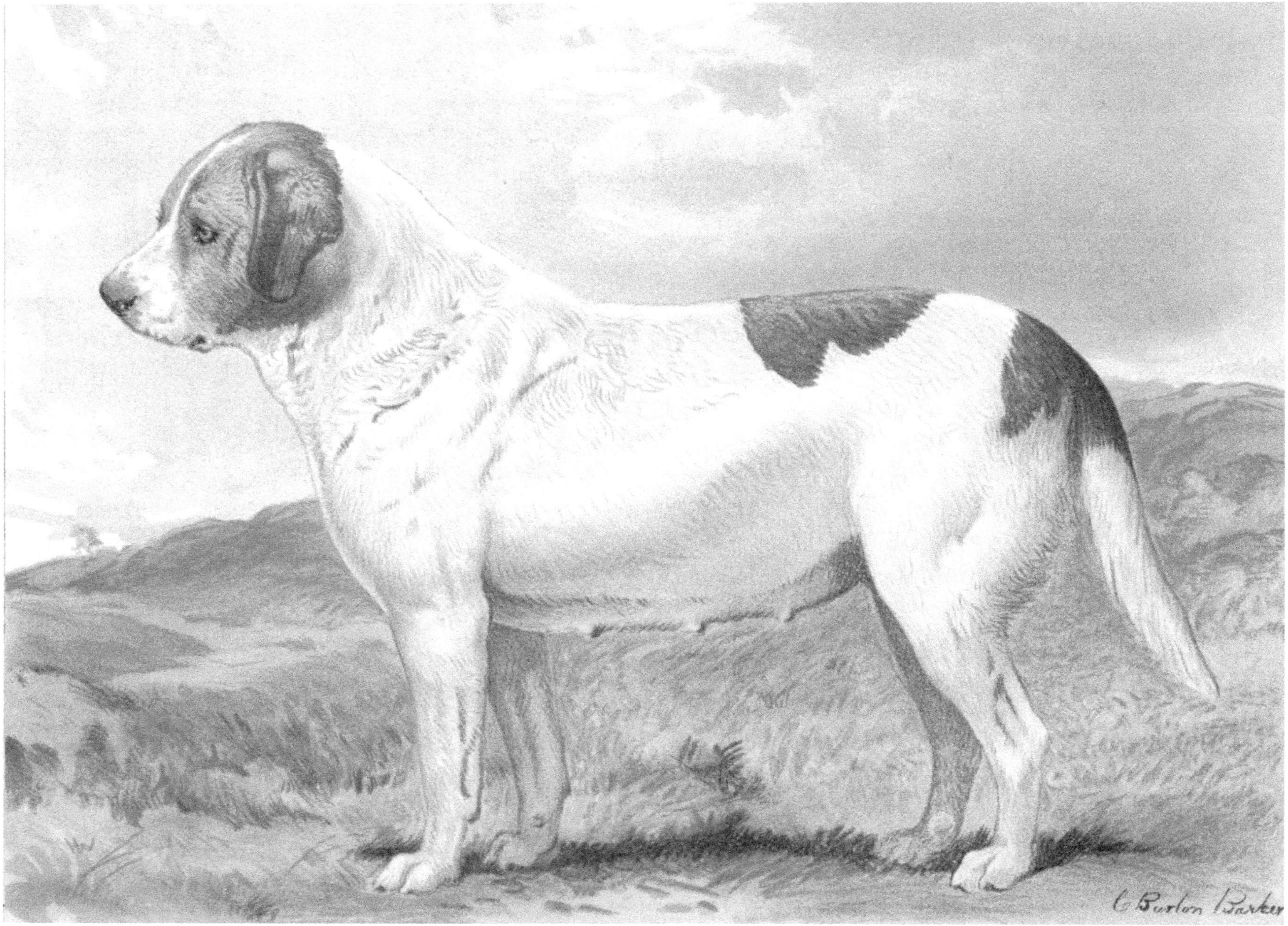
C Burton Barber

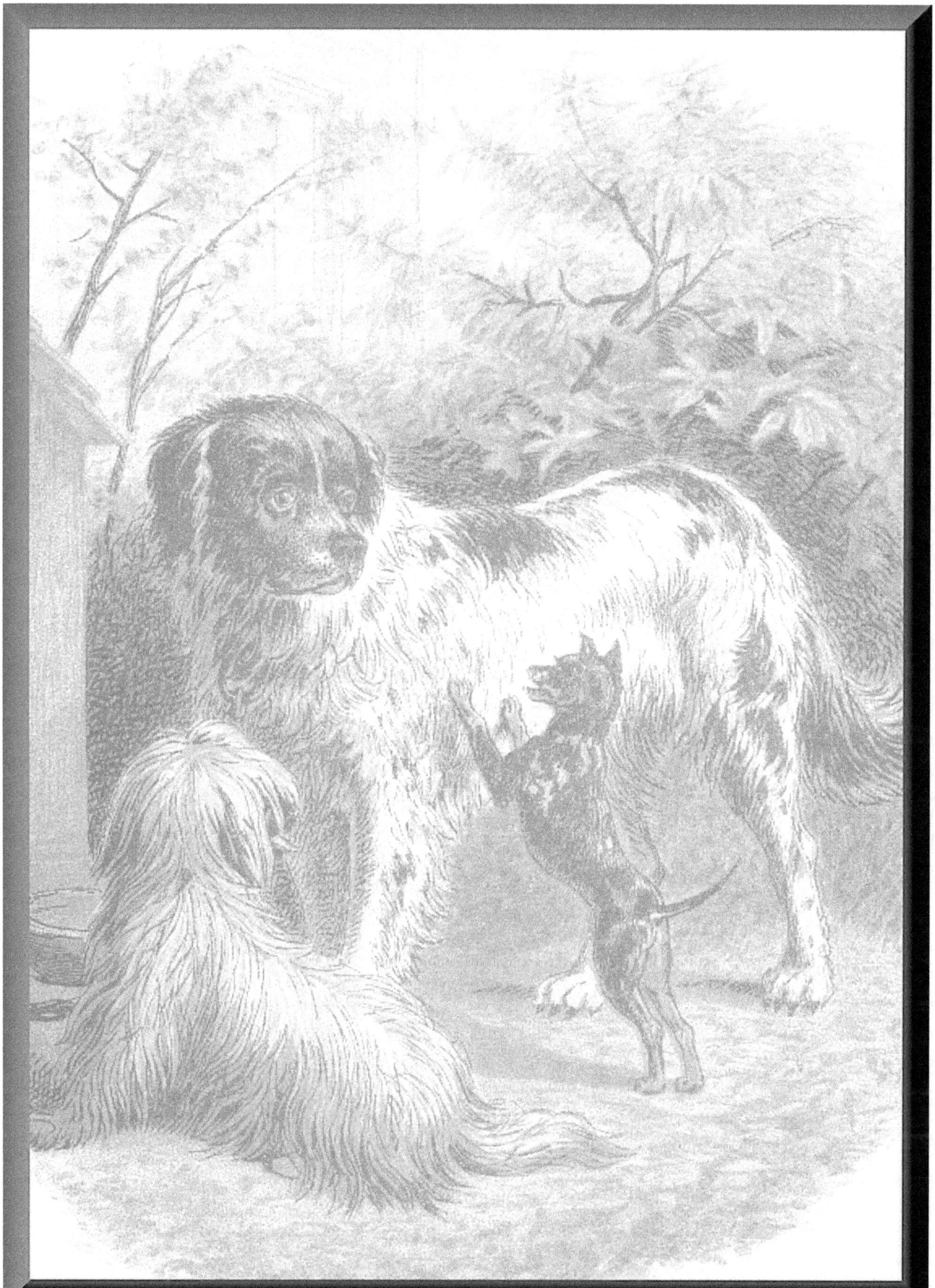

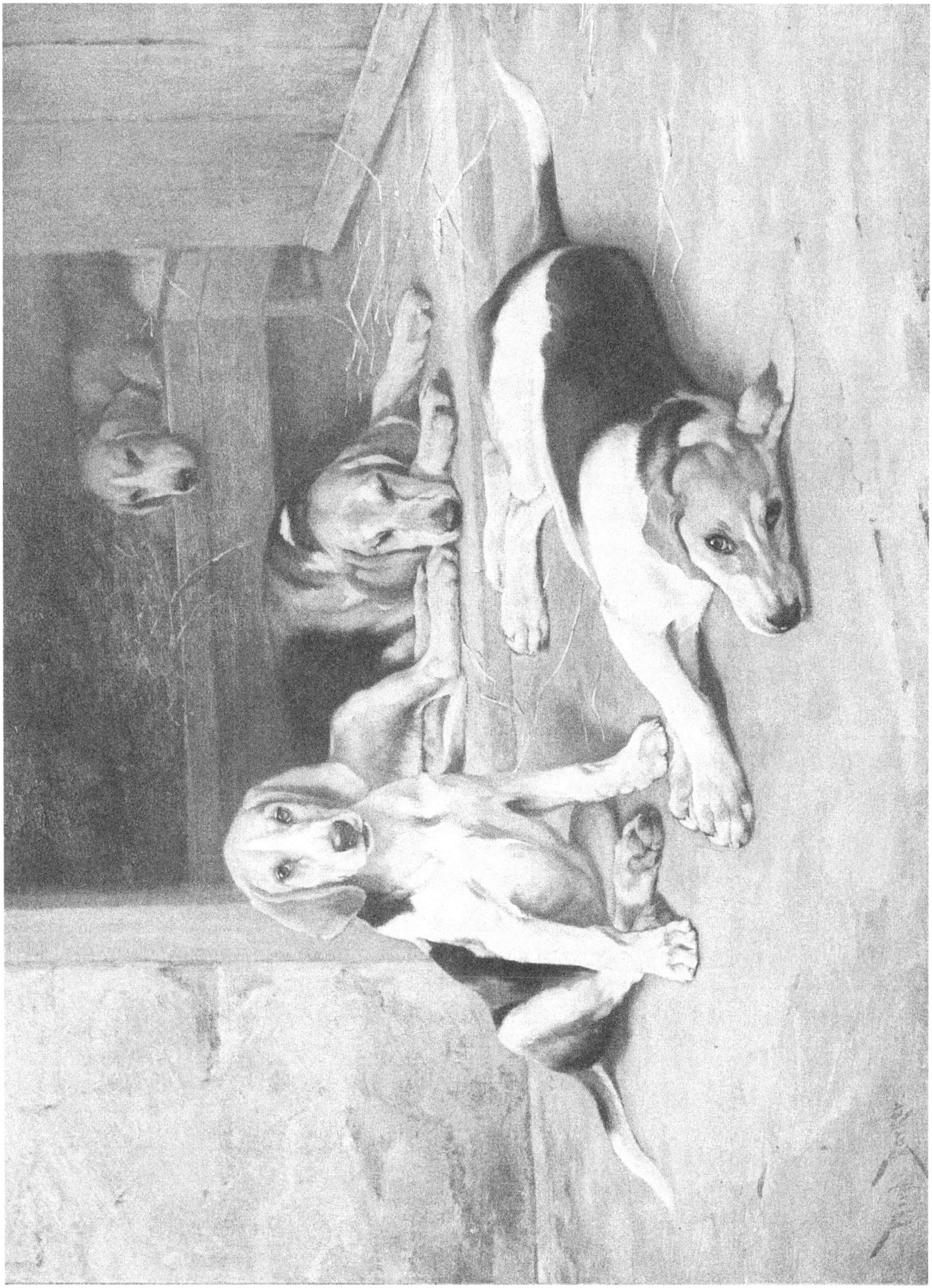

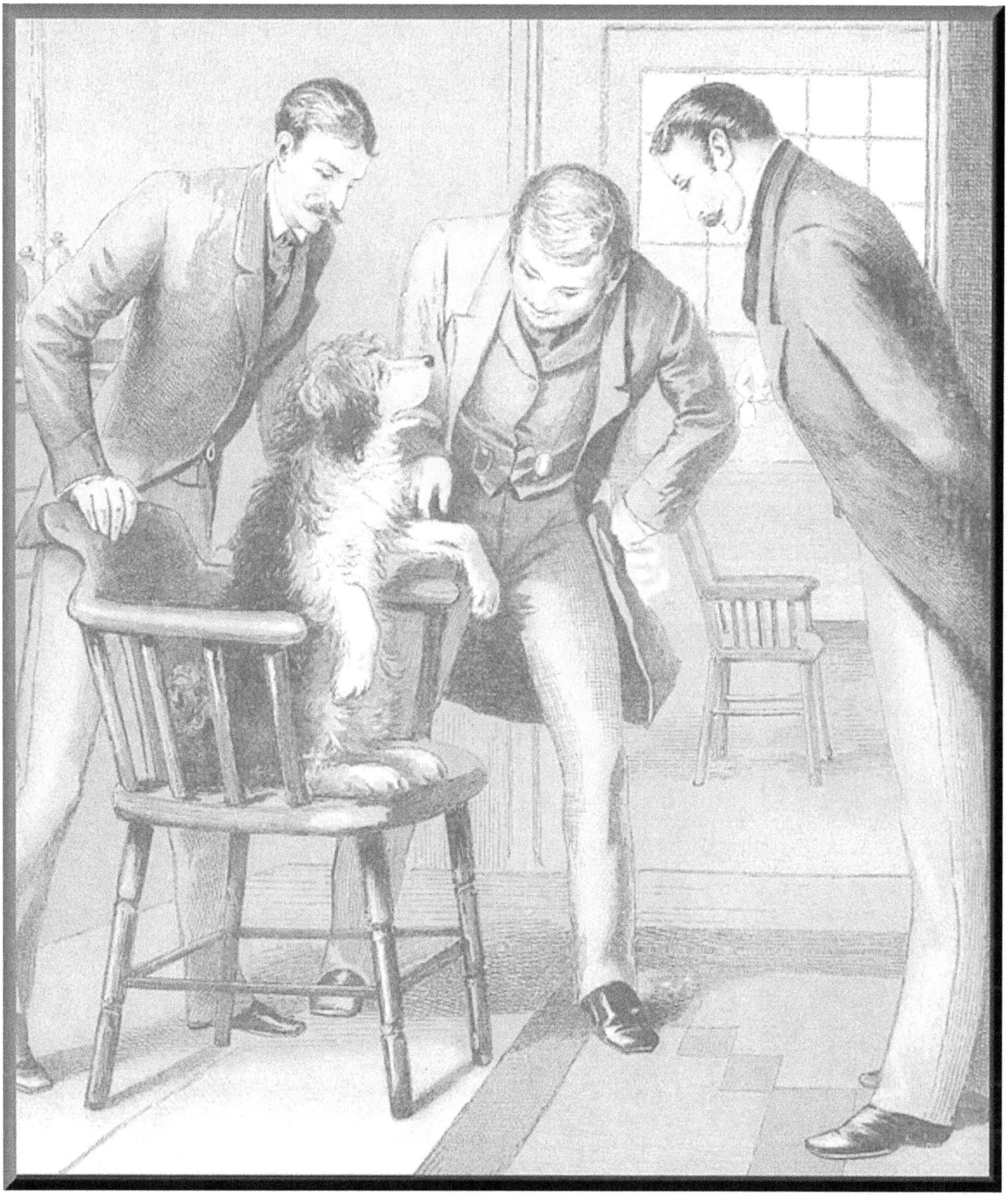

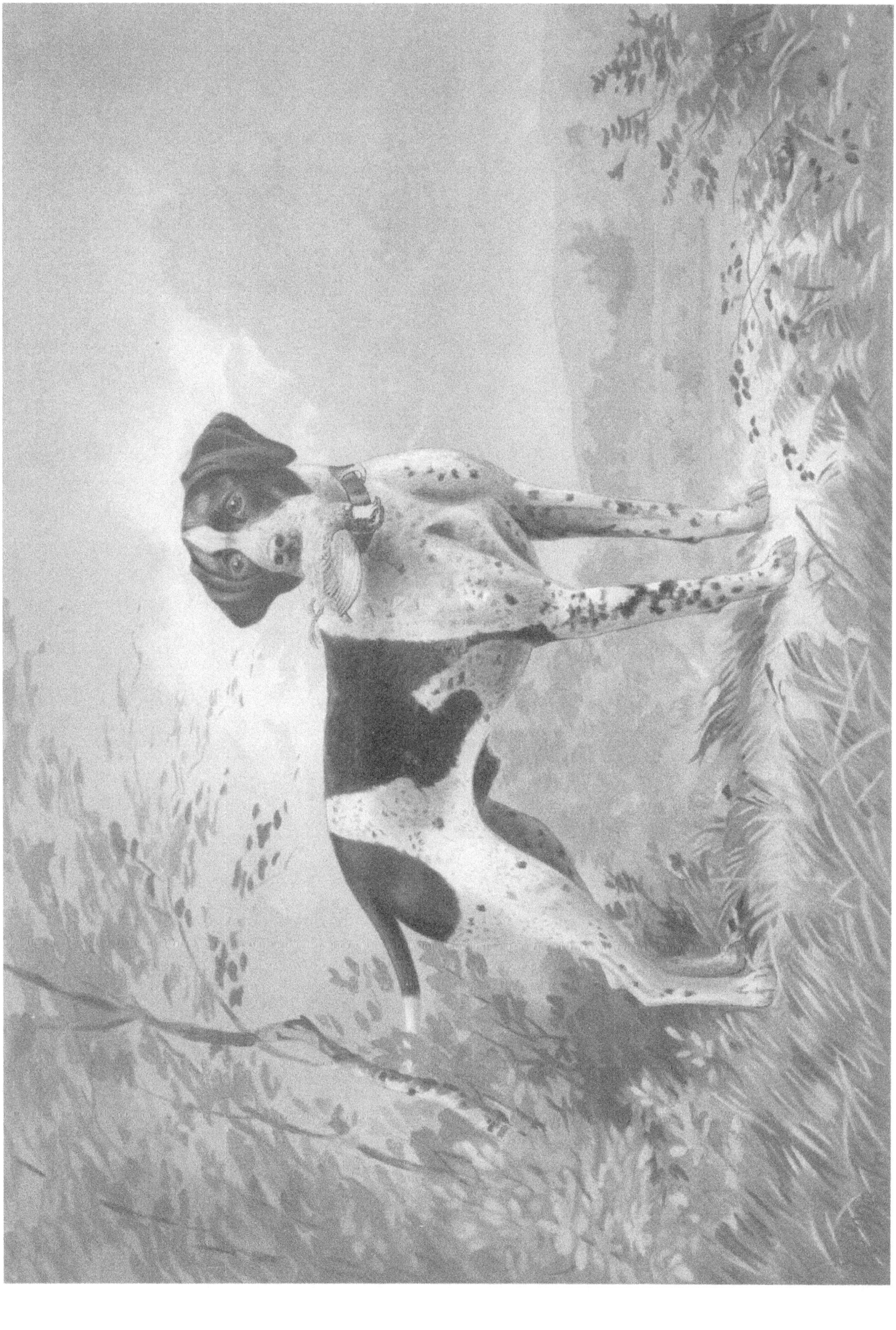

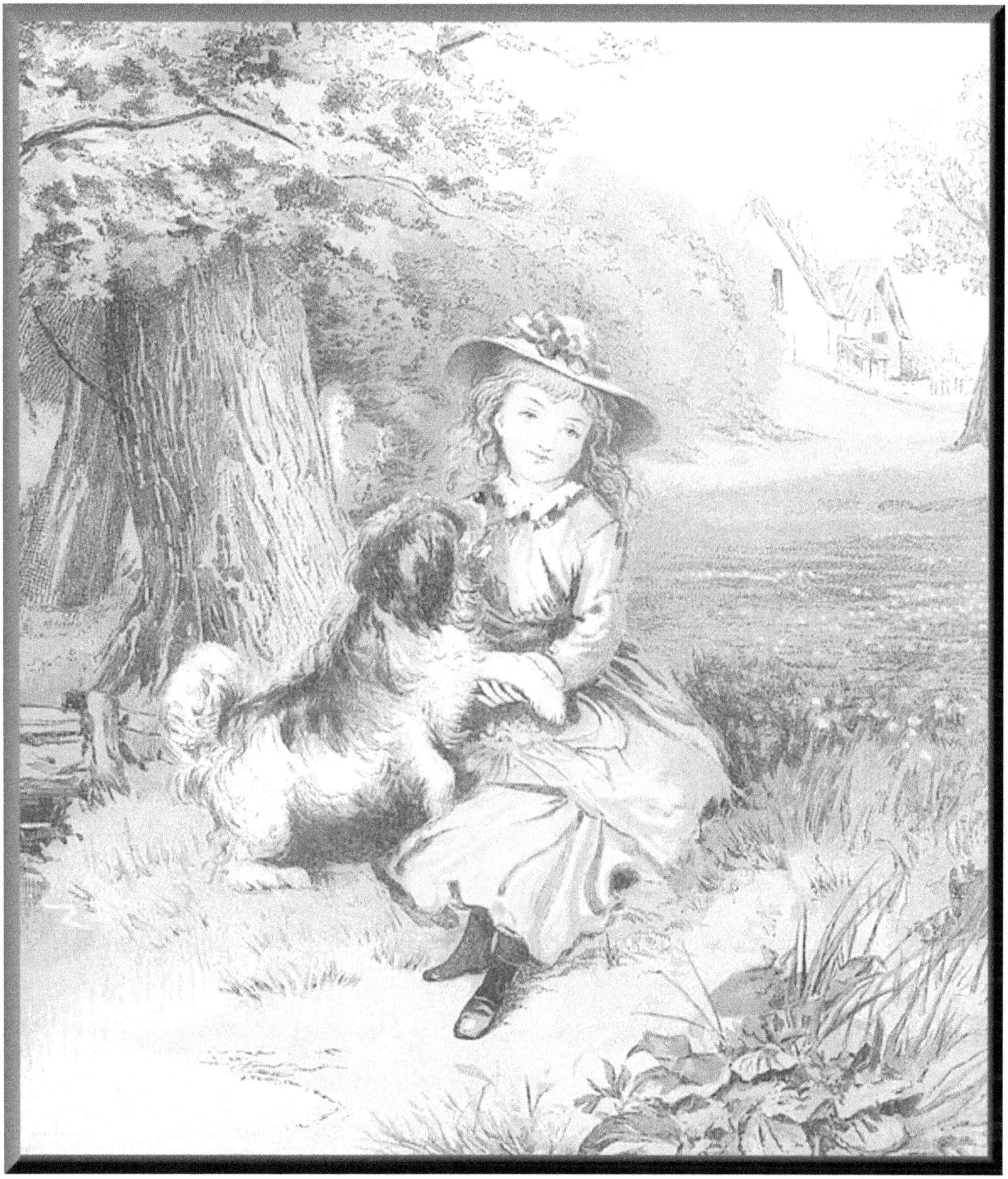

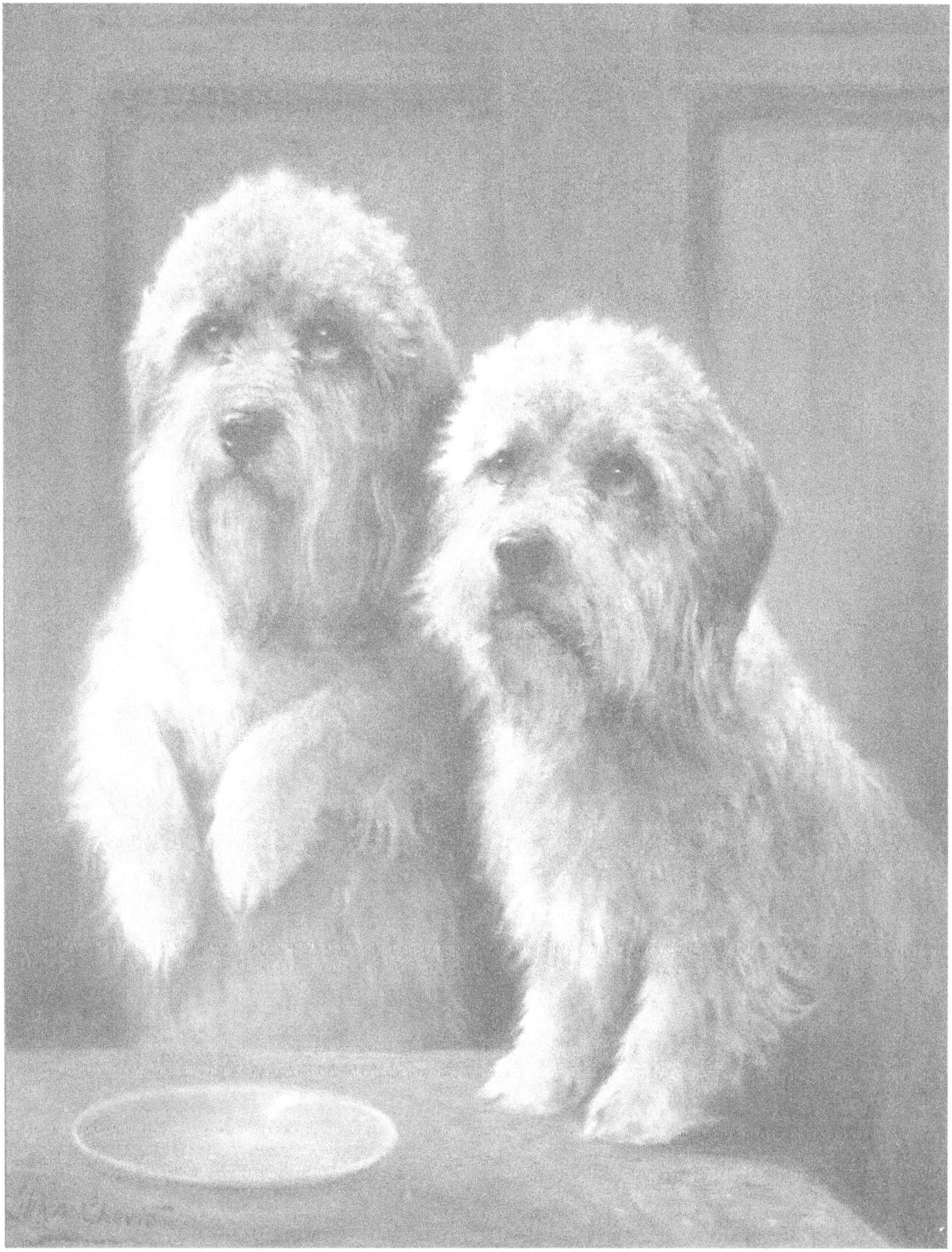

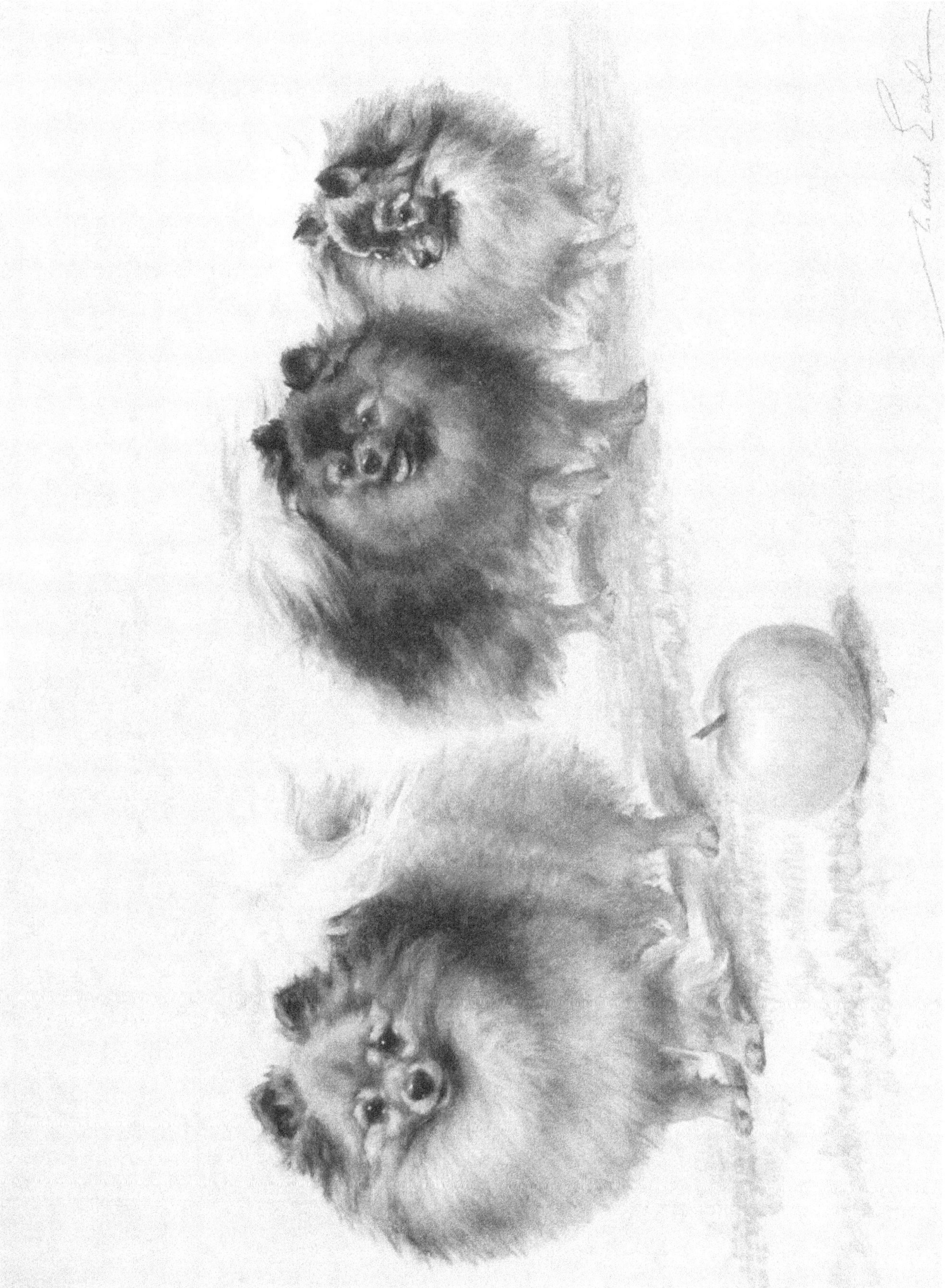

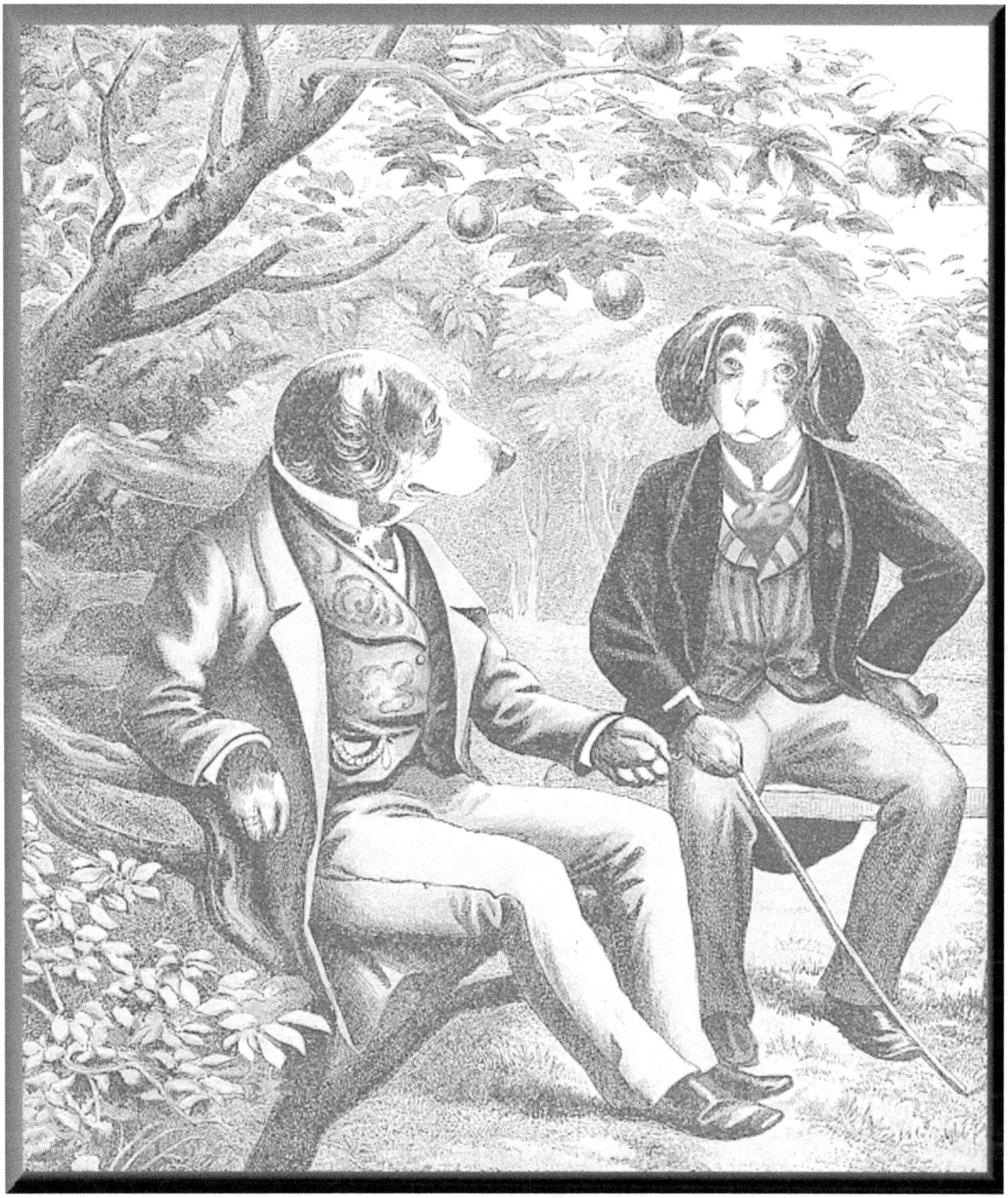

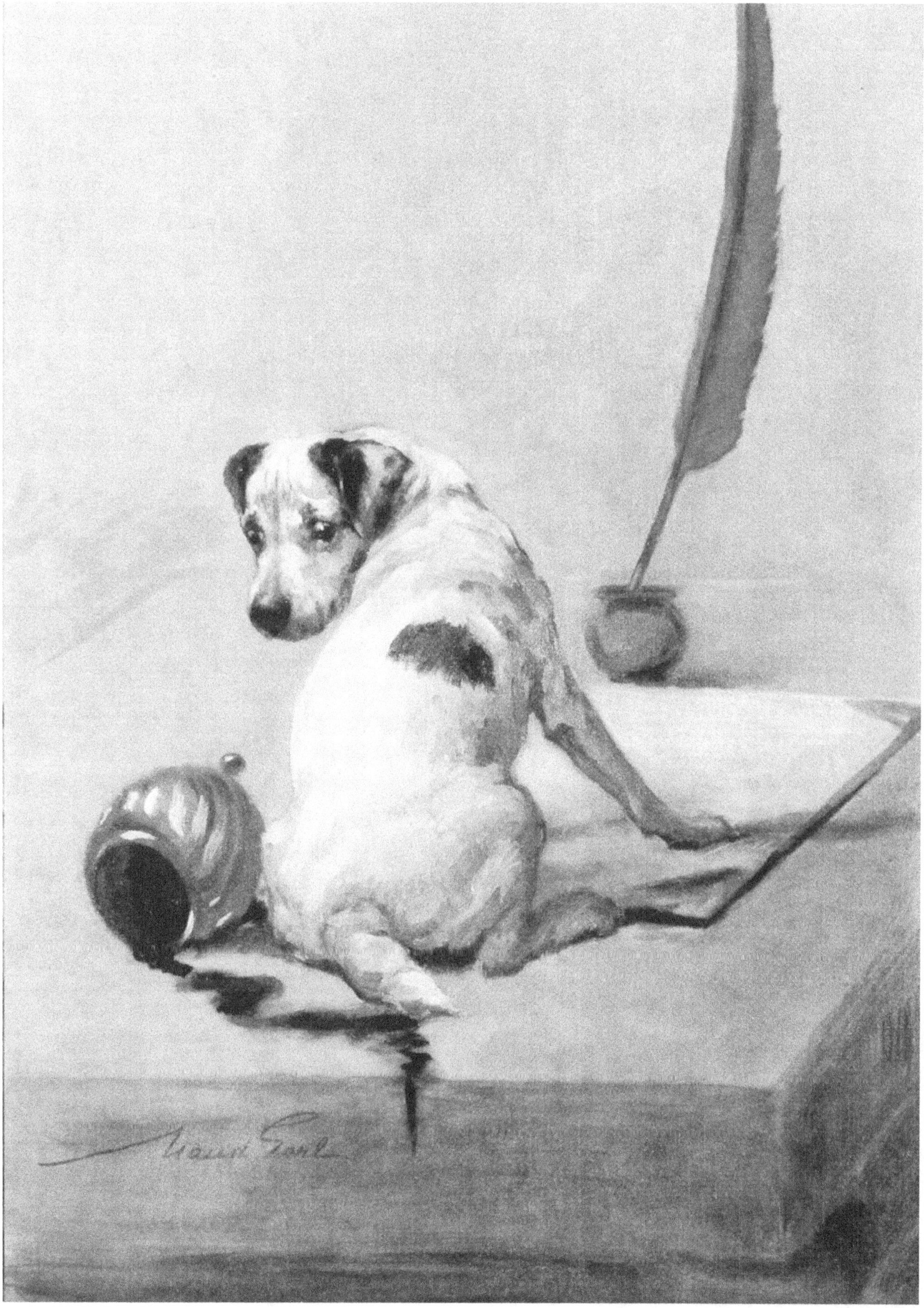

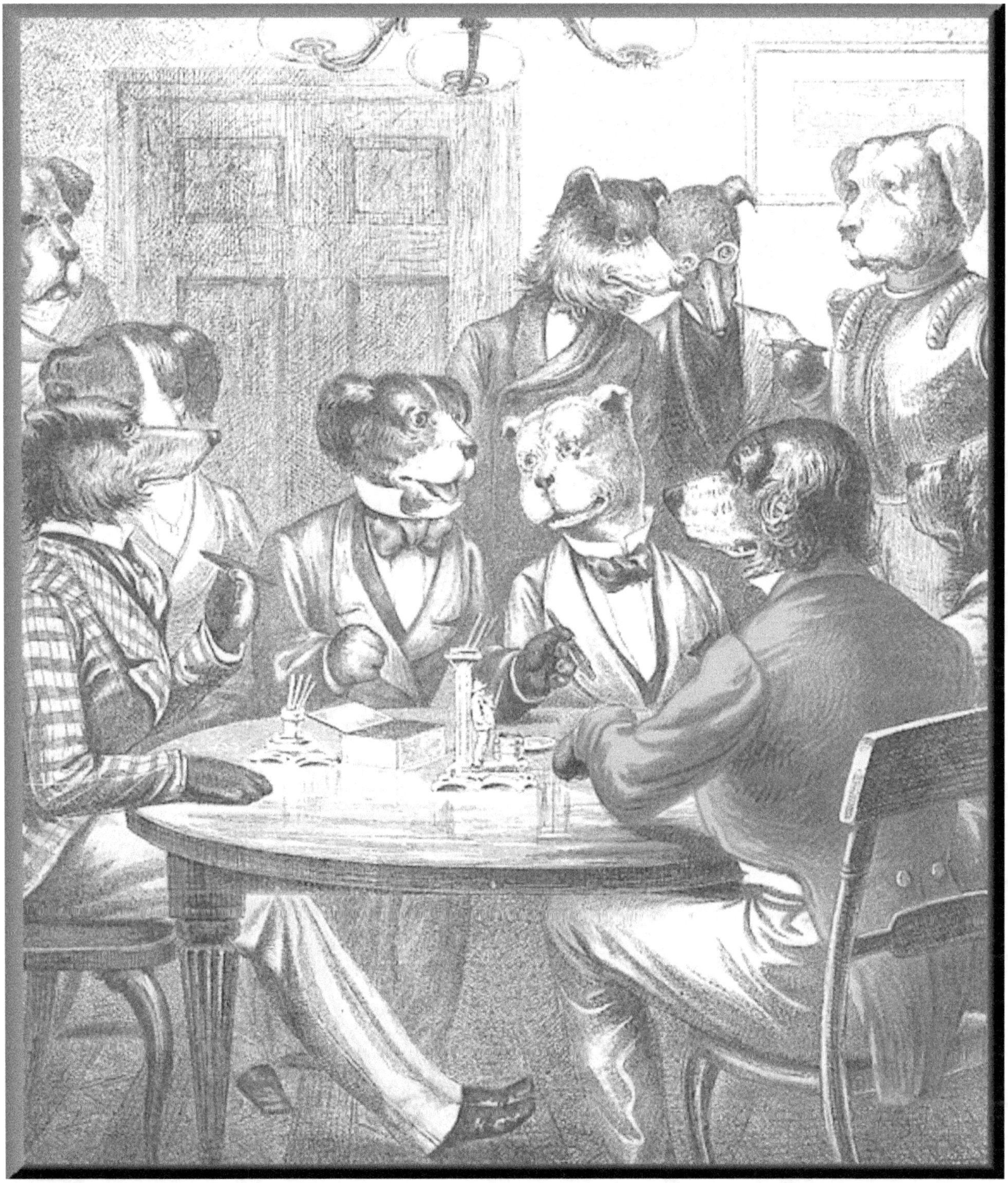

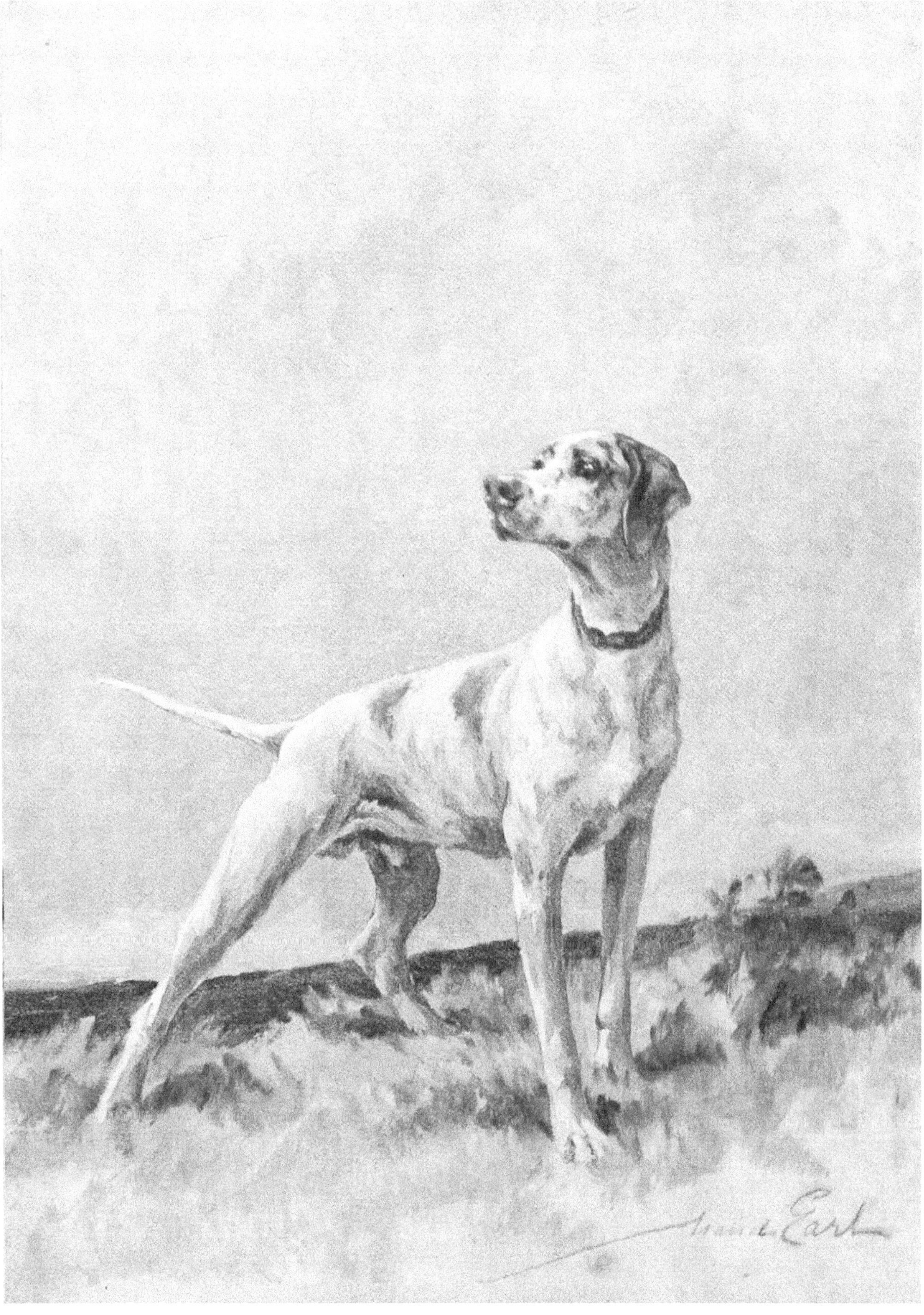

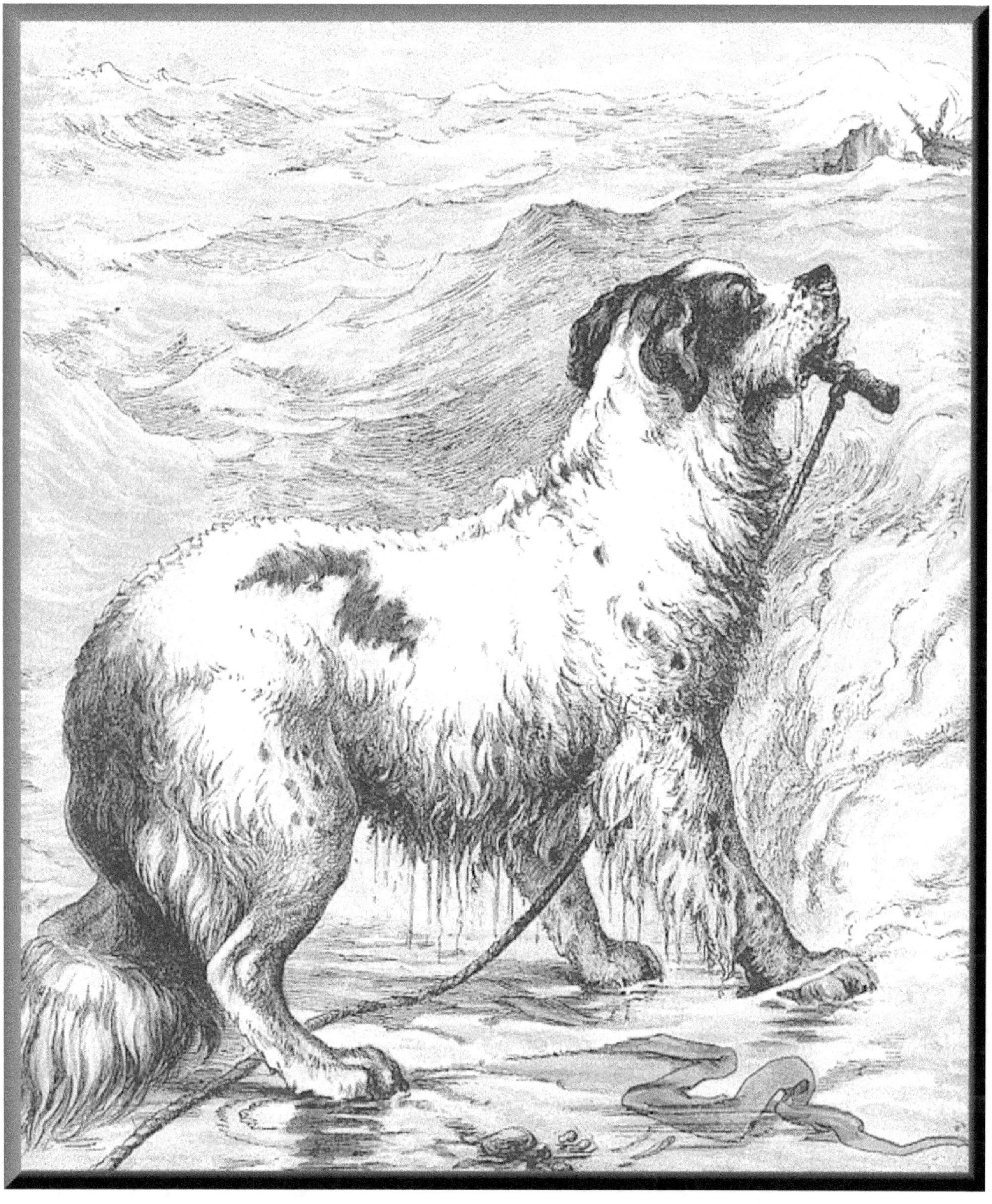

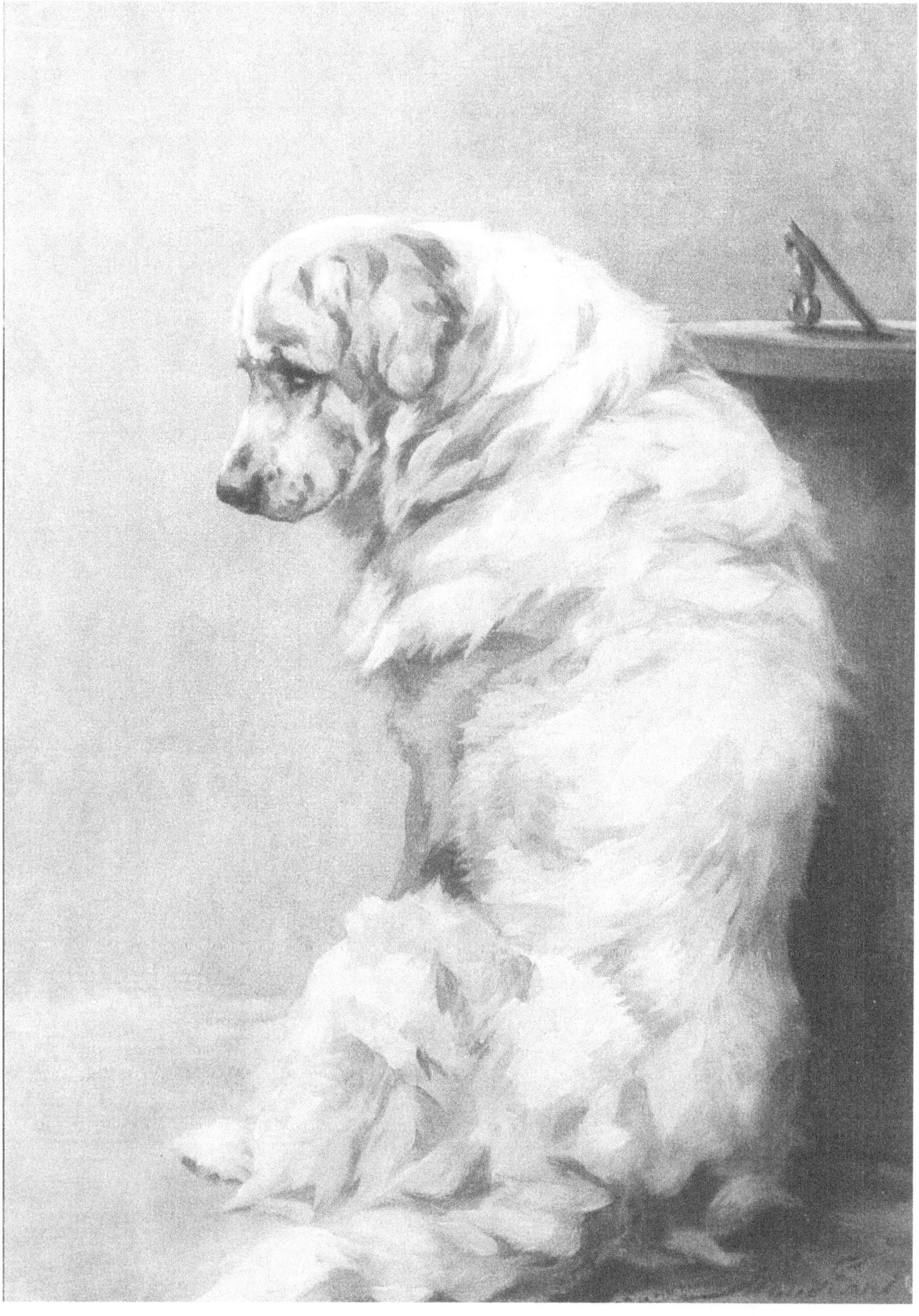

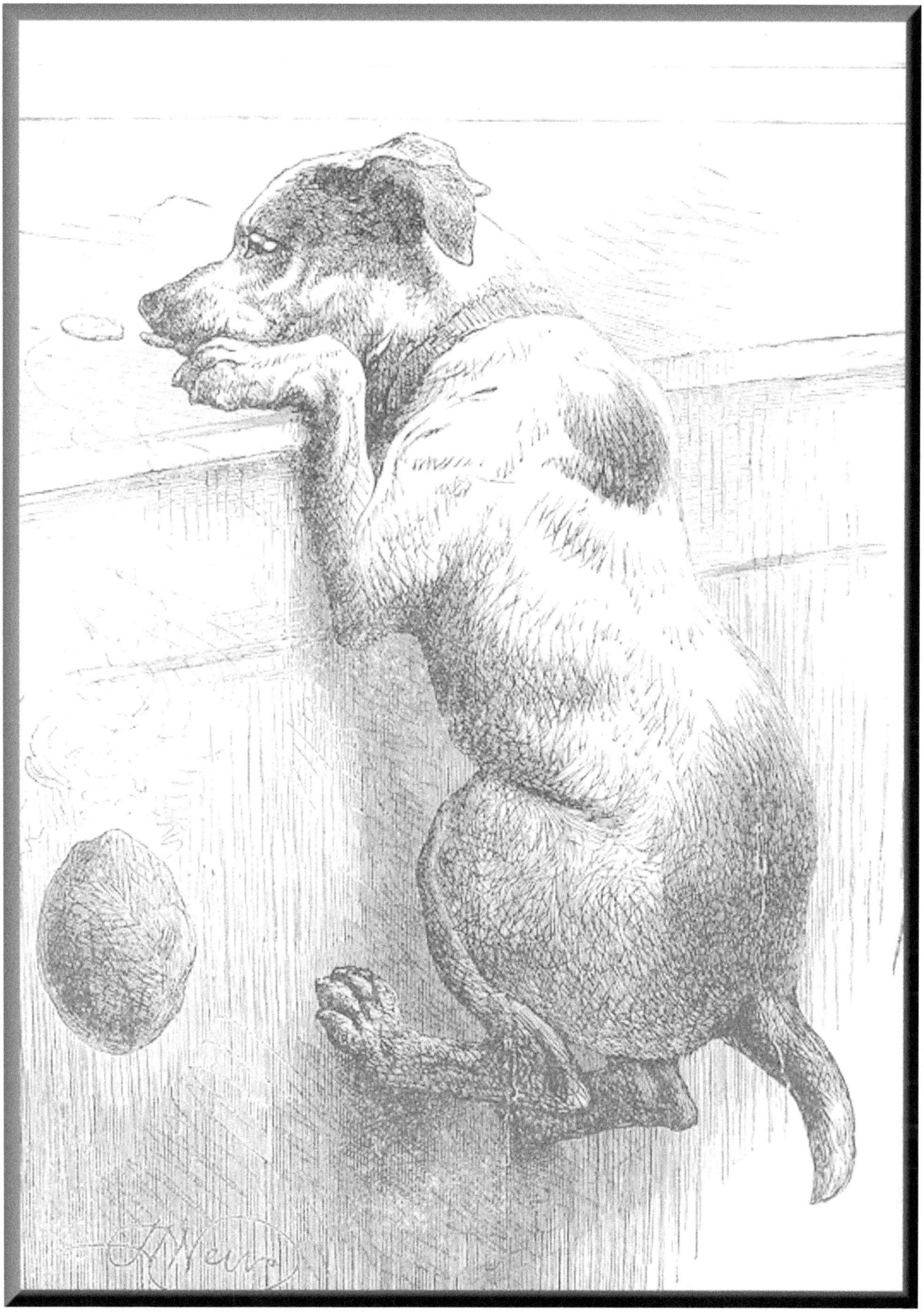

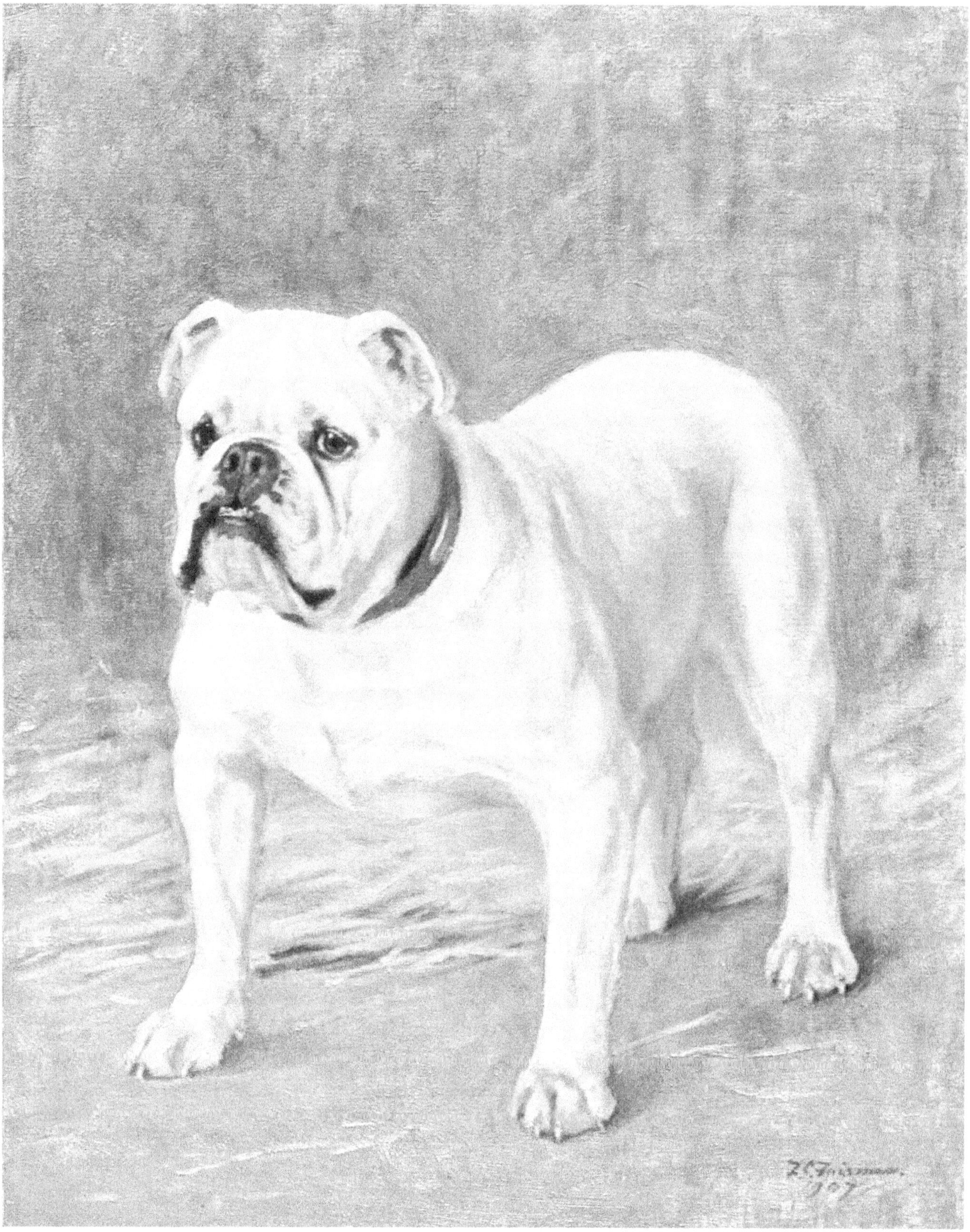

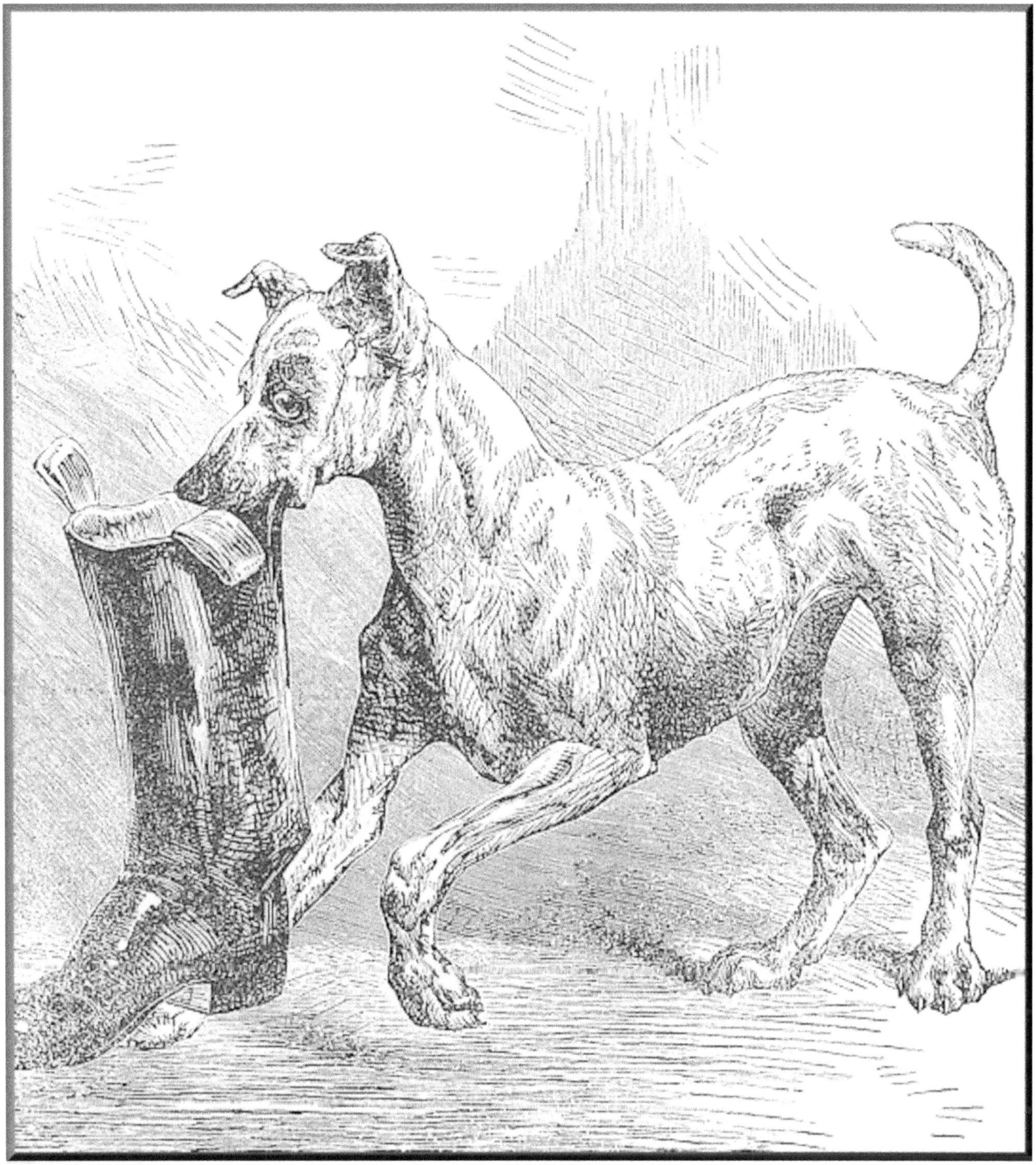

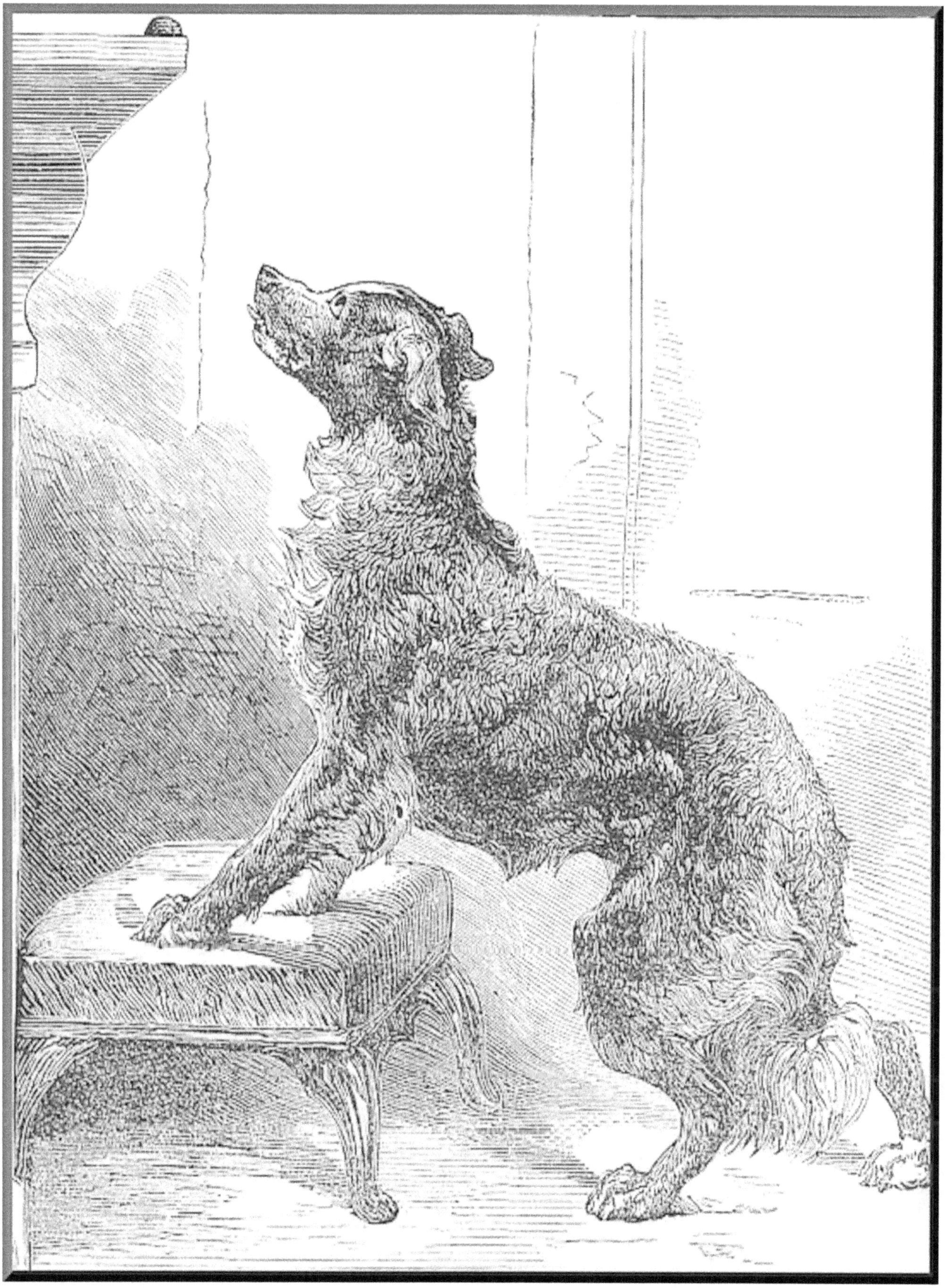

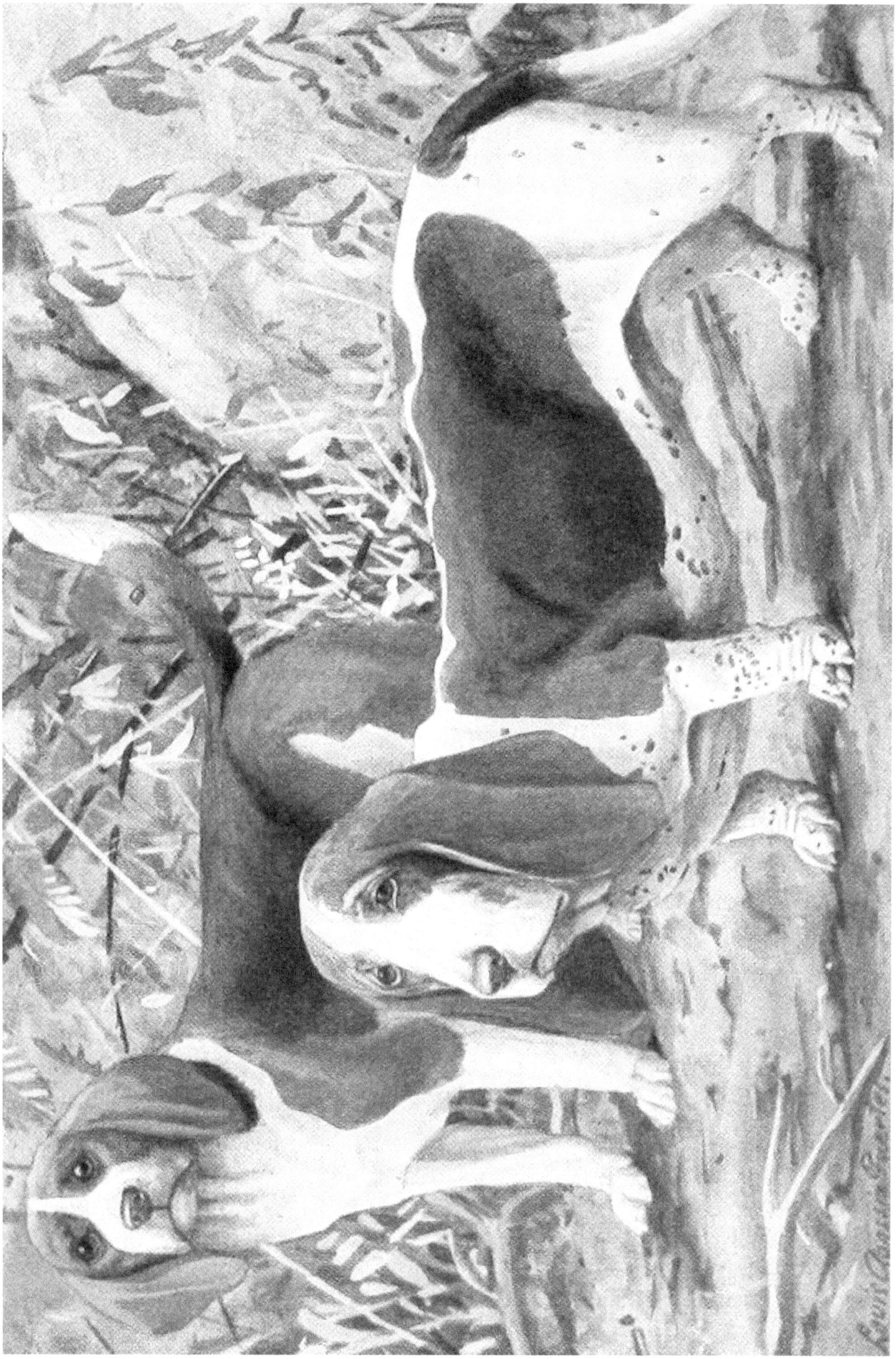

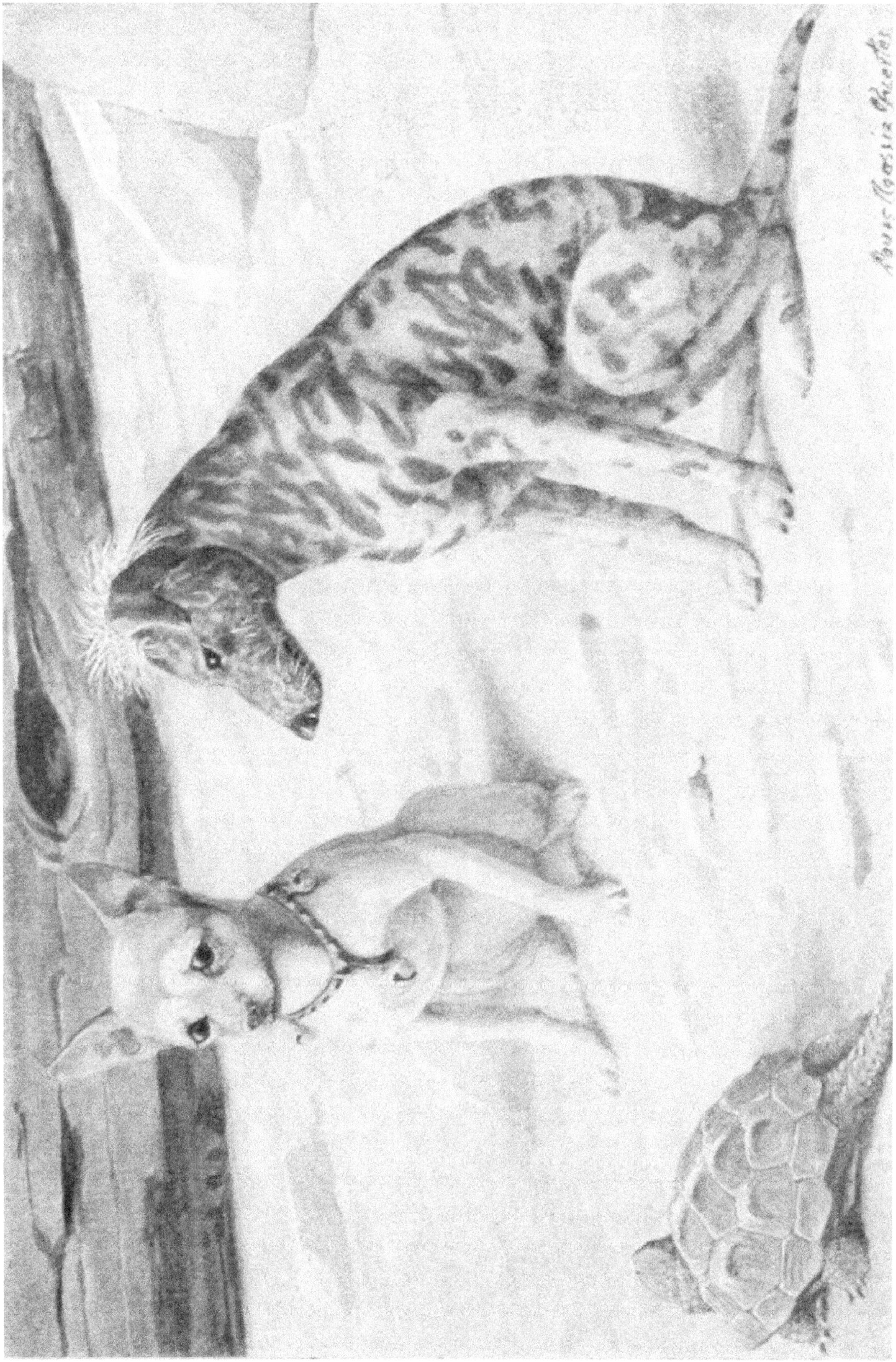

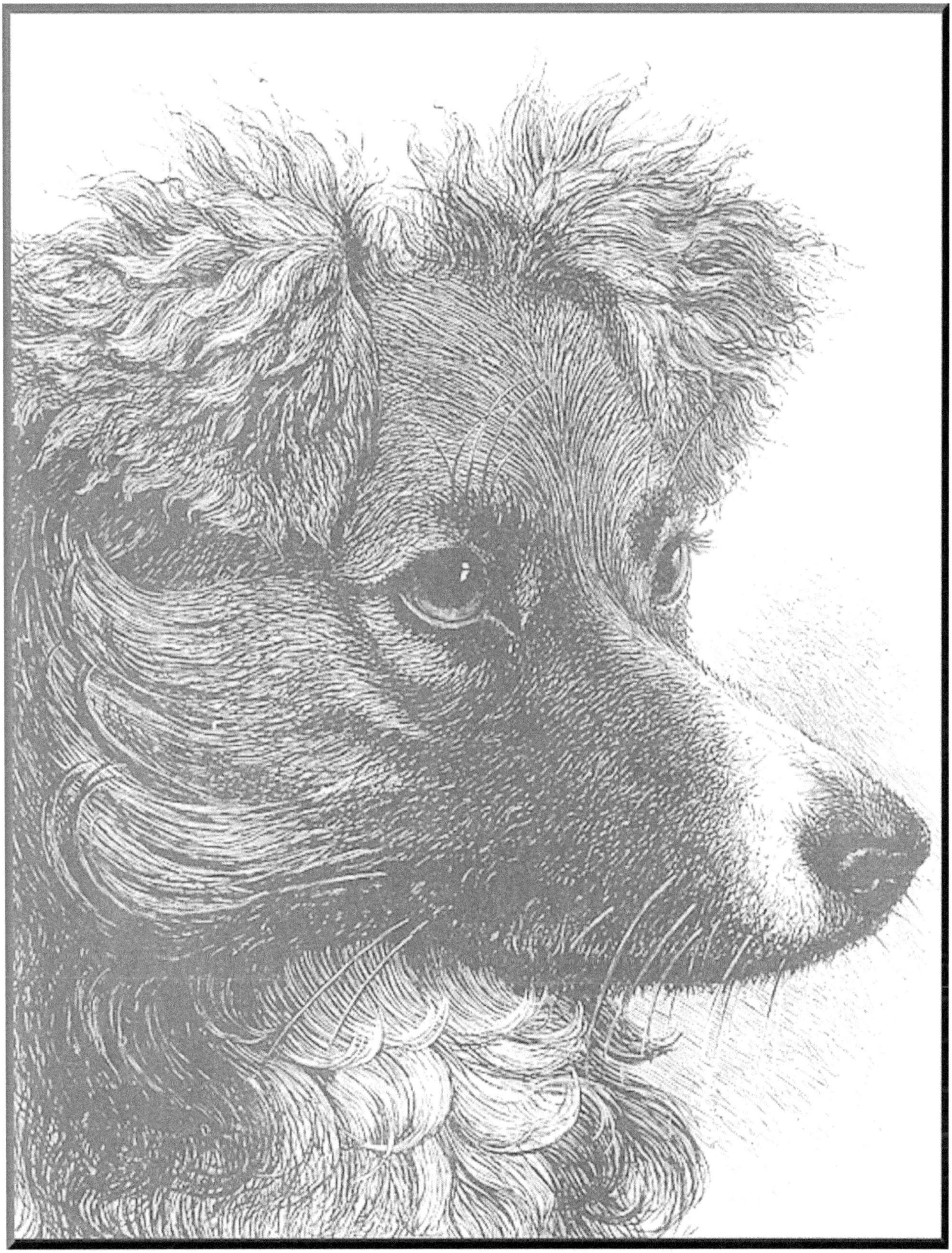

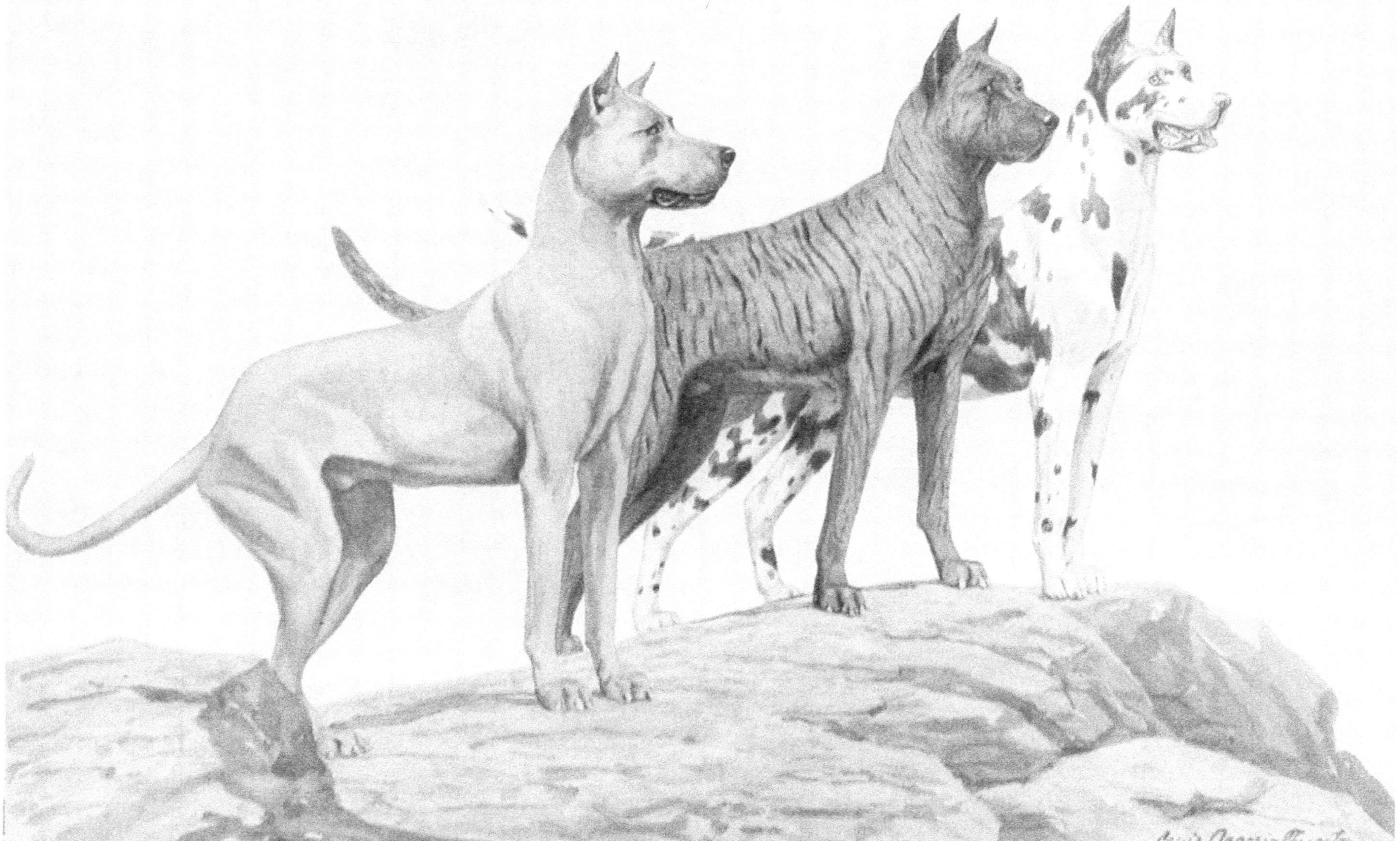
Louis Agassiz Fuertes.

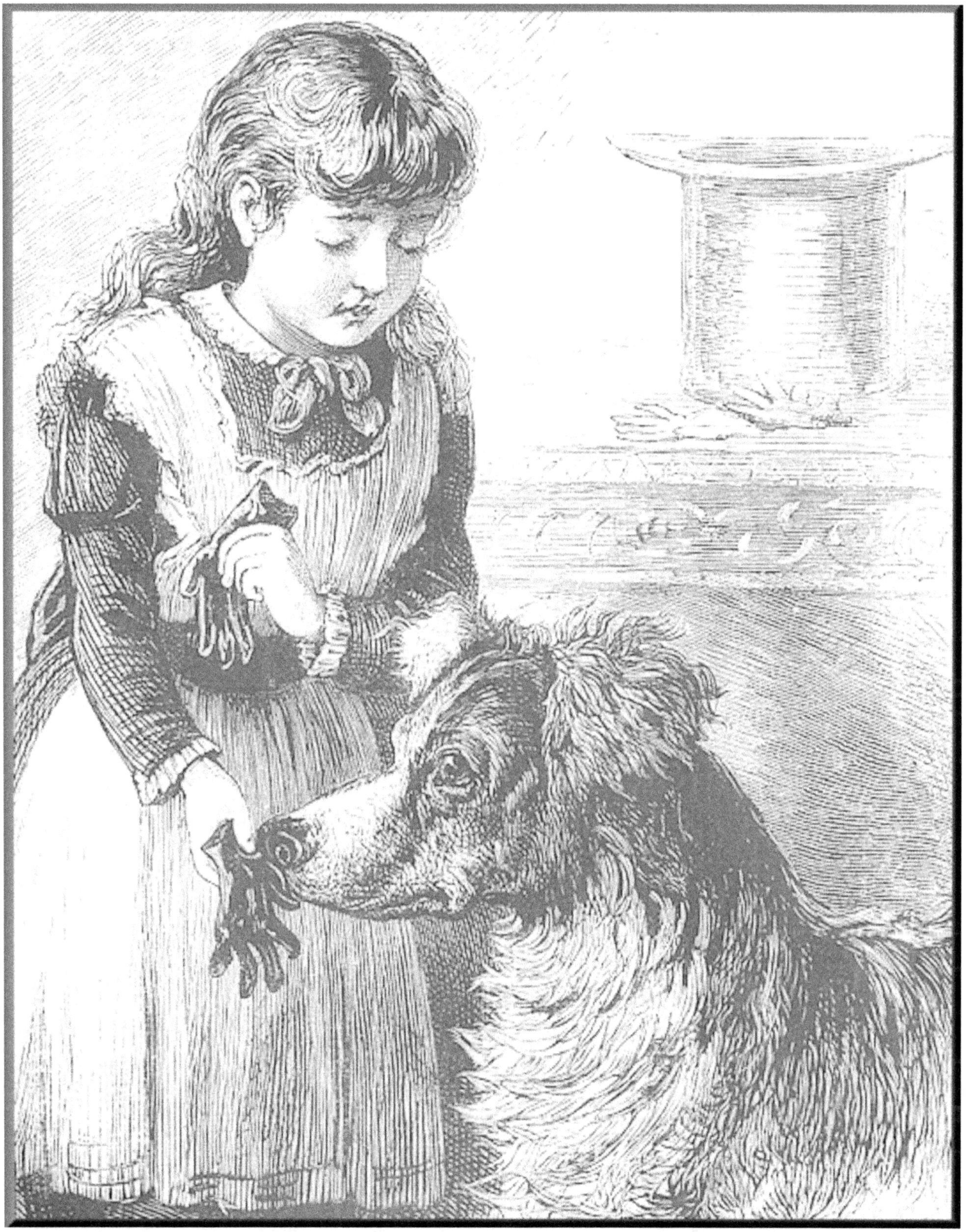

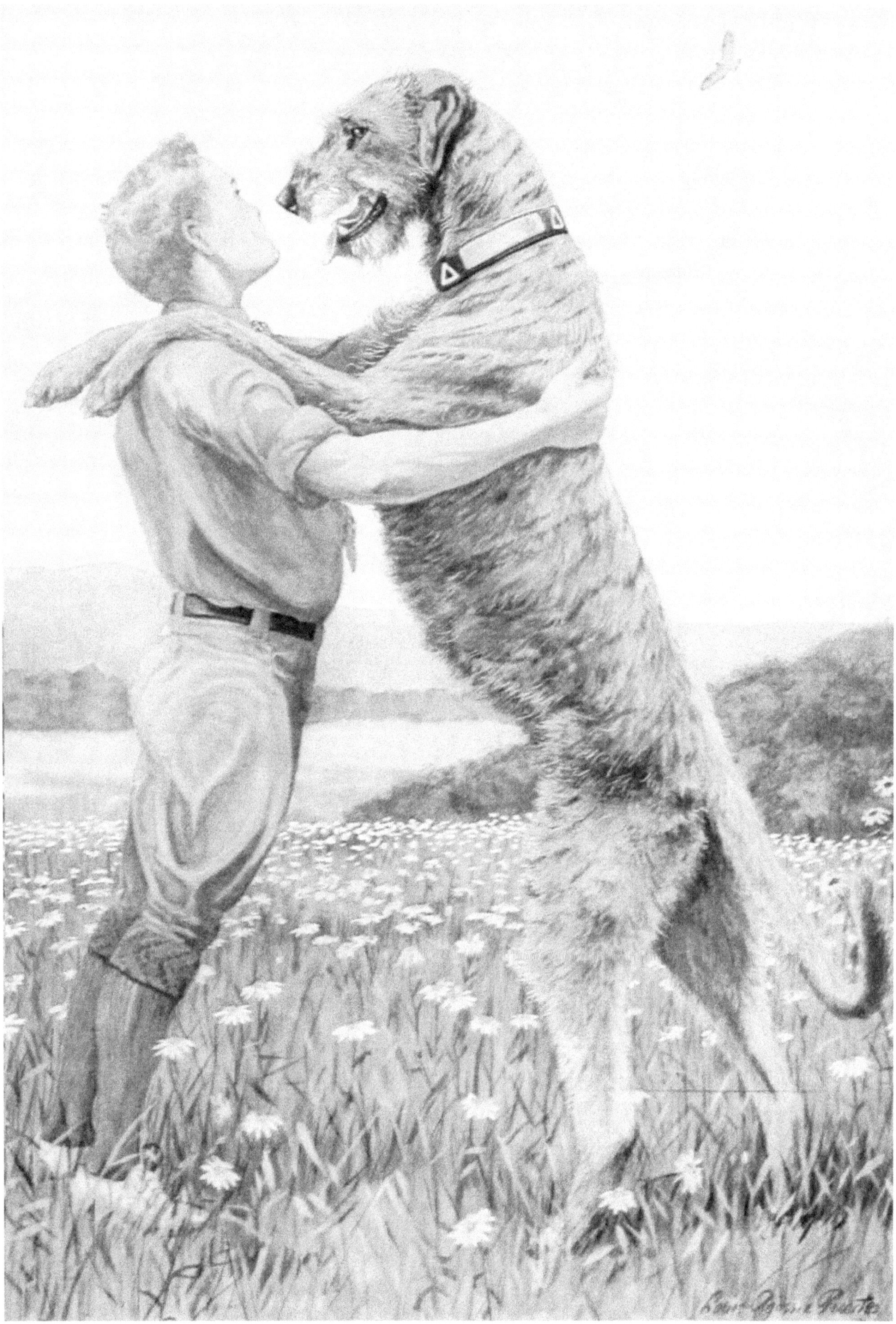

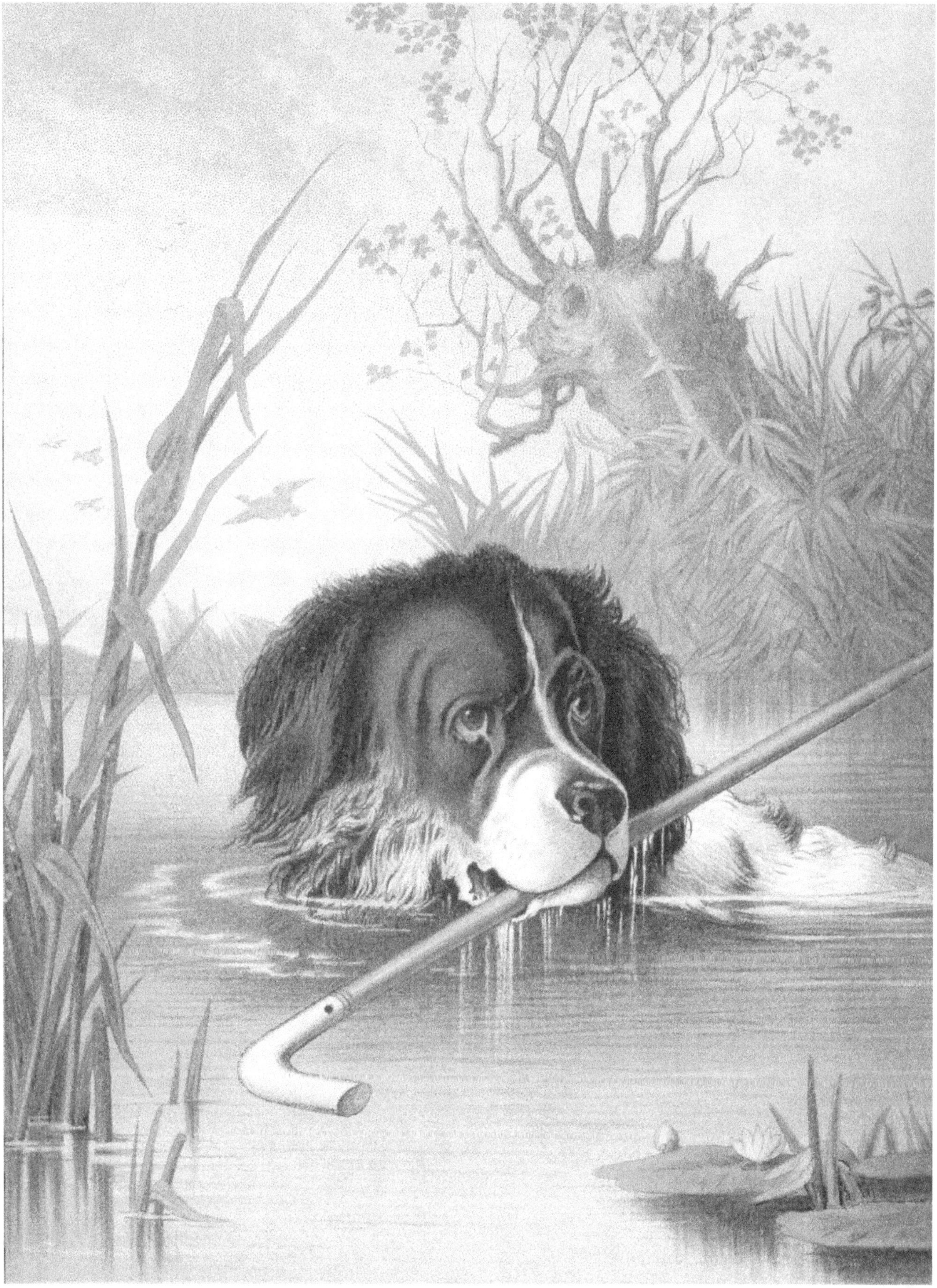

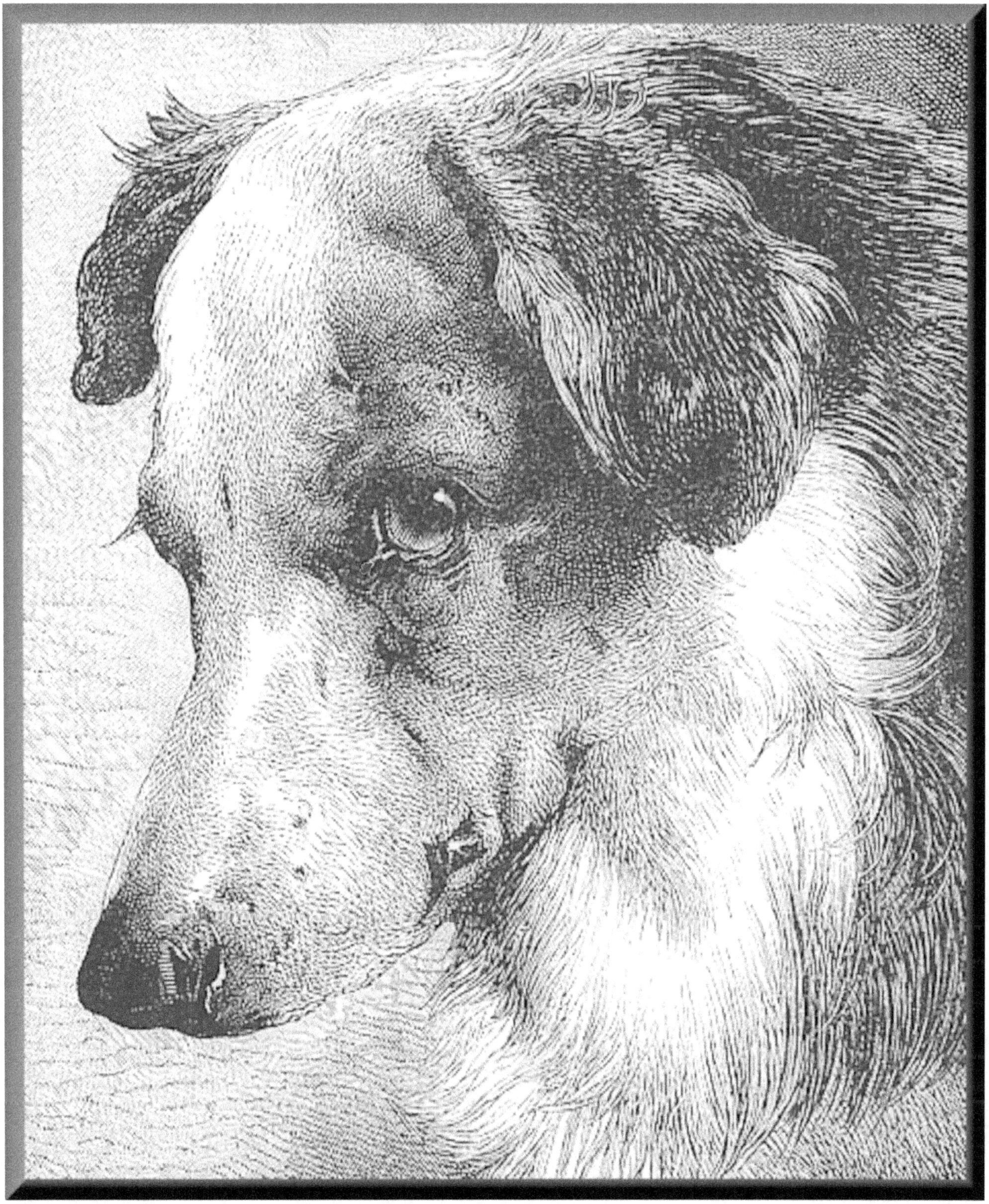

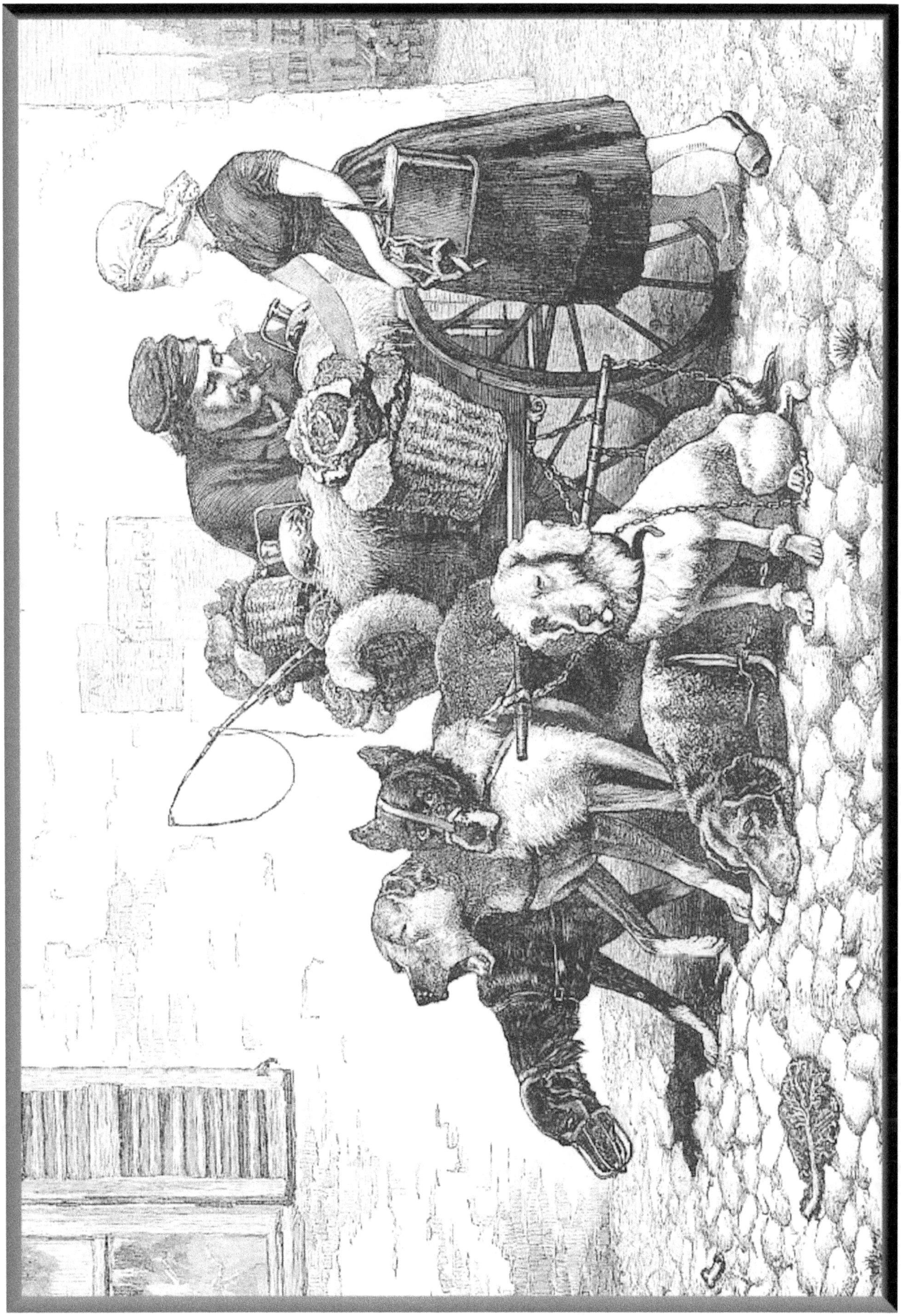

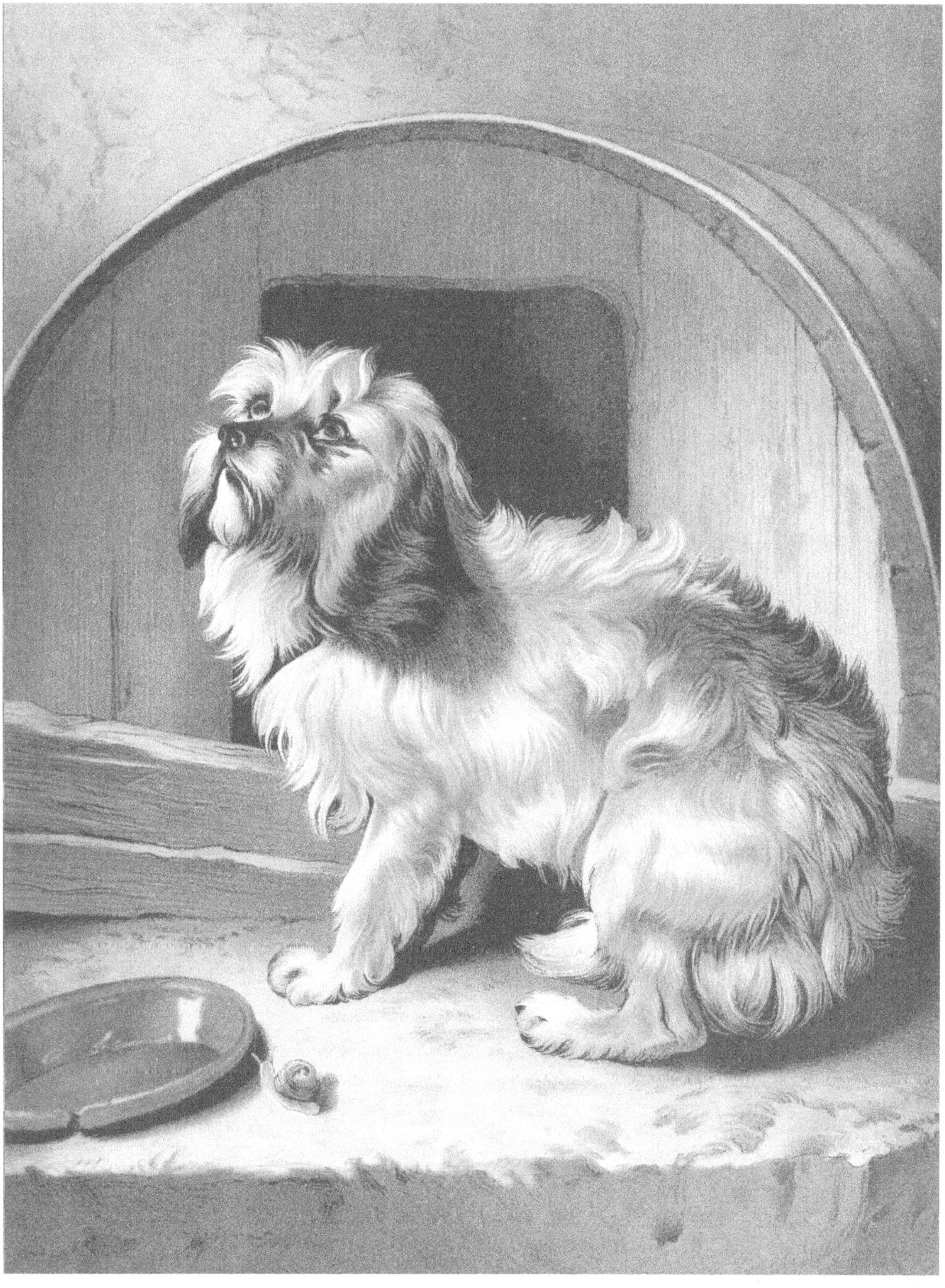

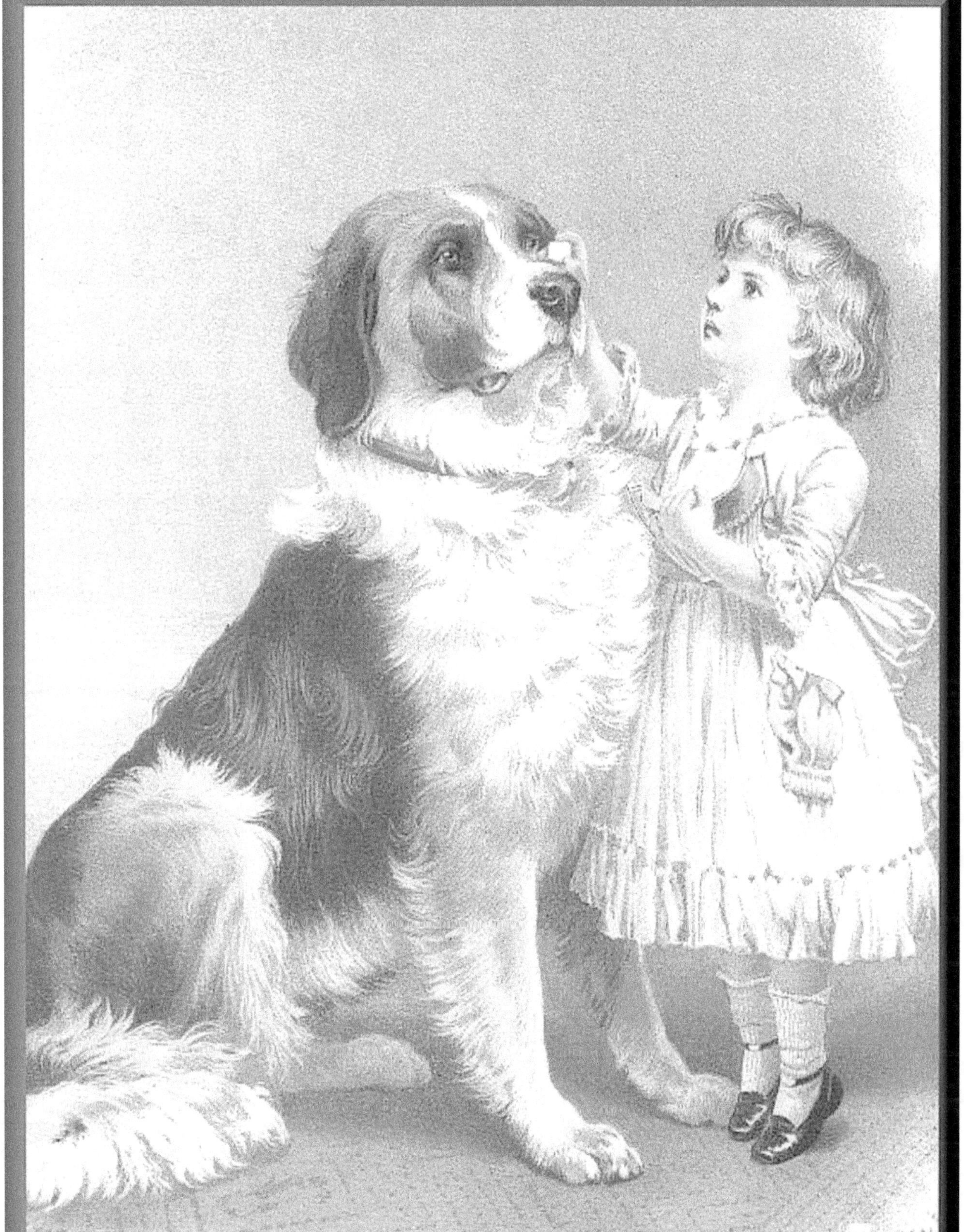

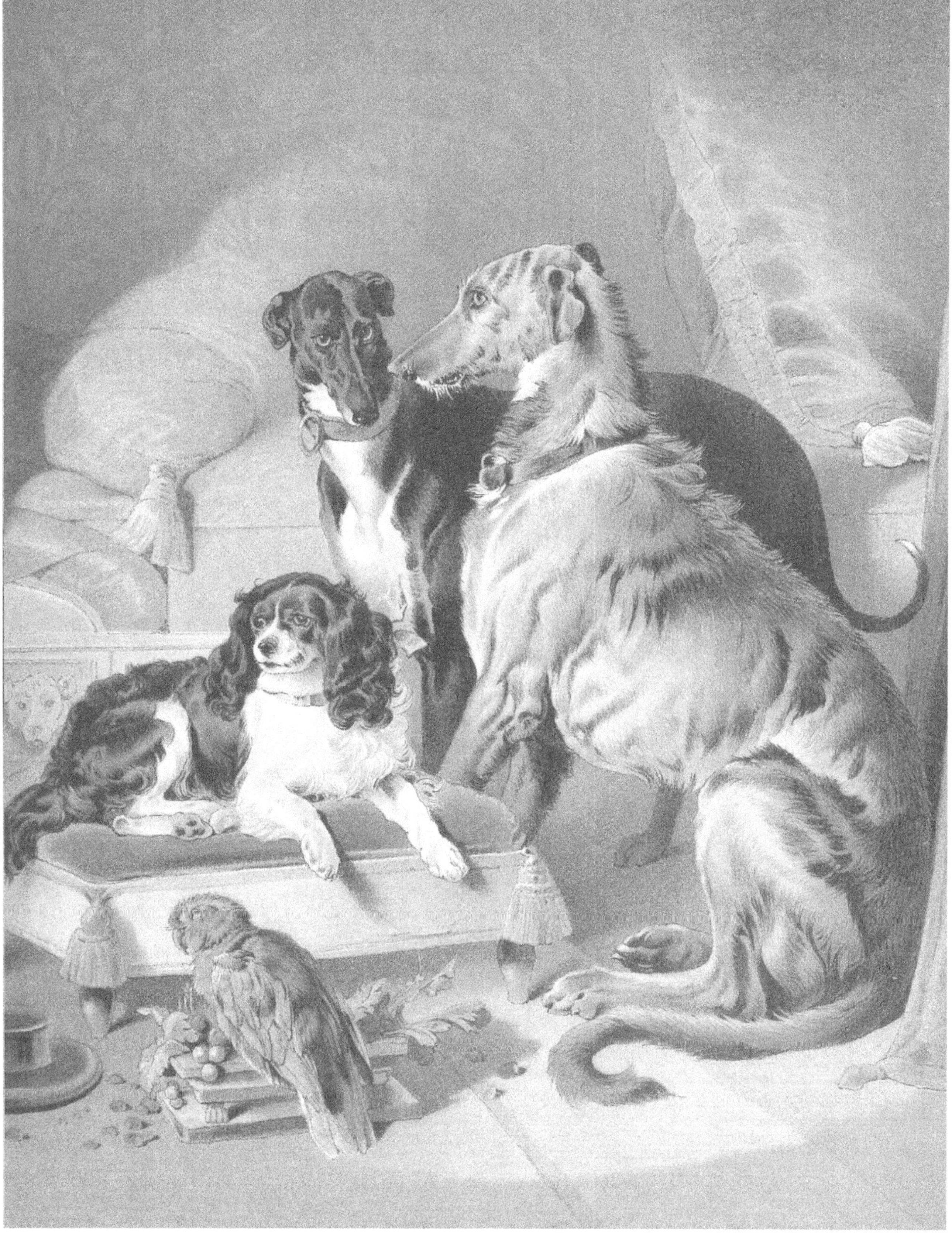

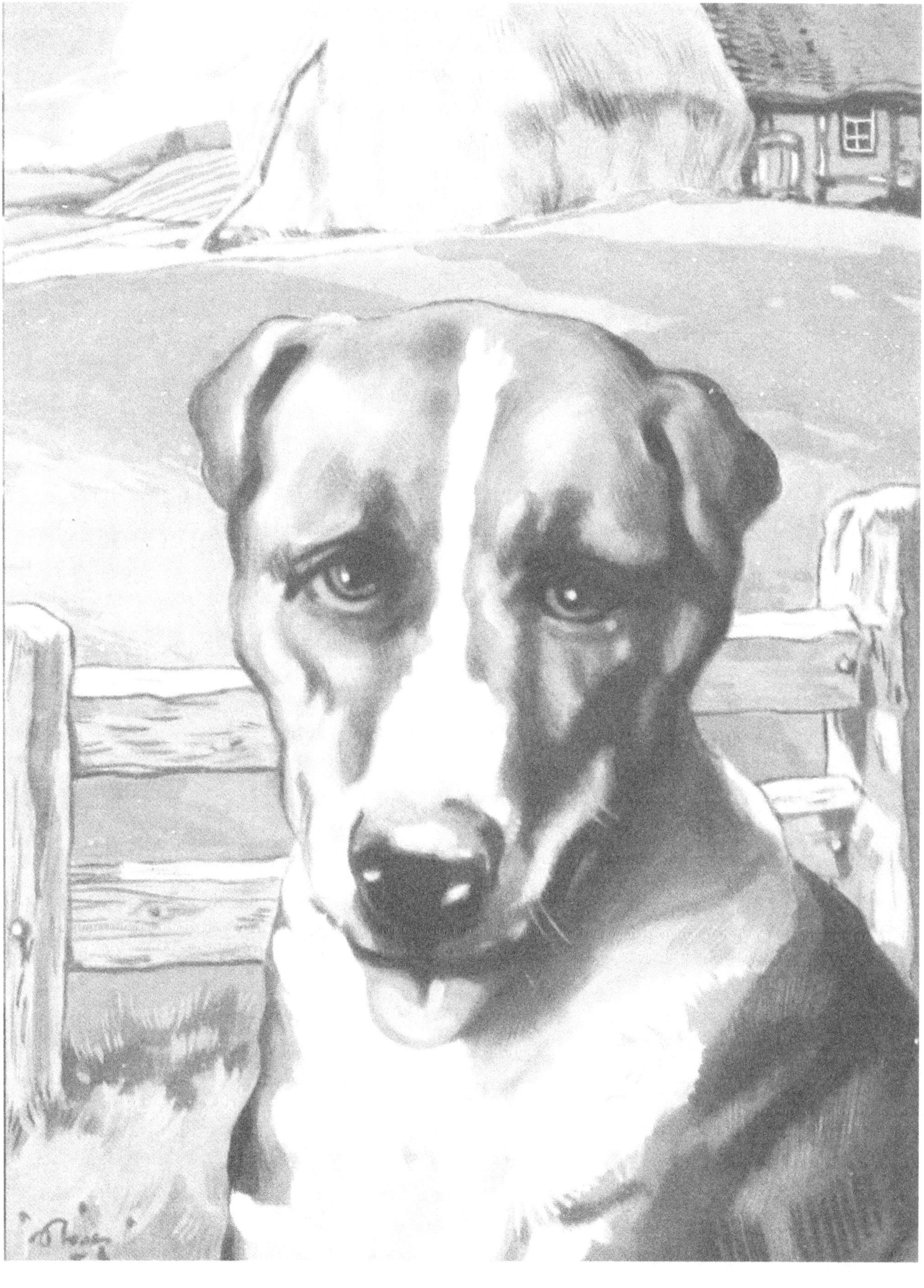

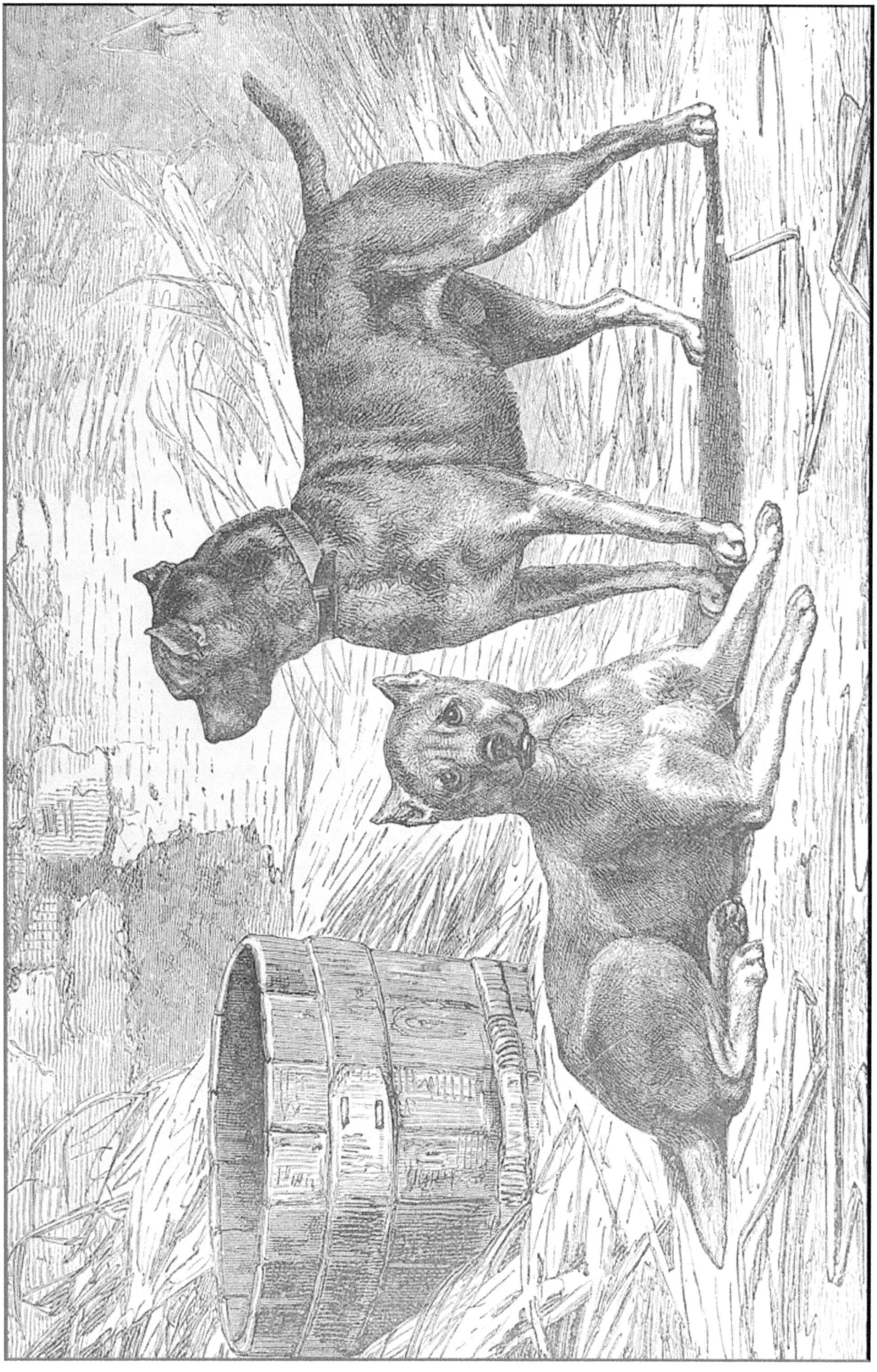

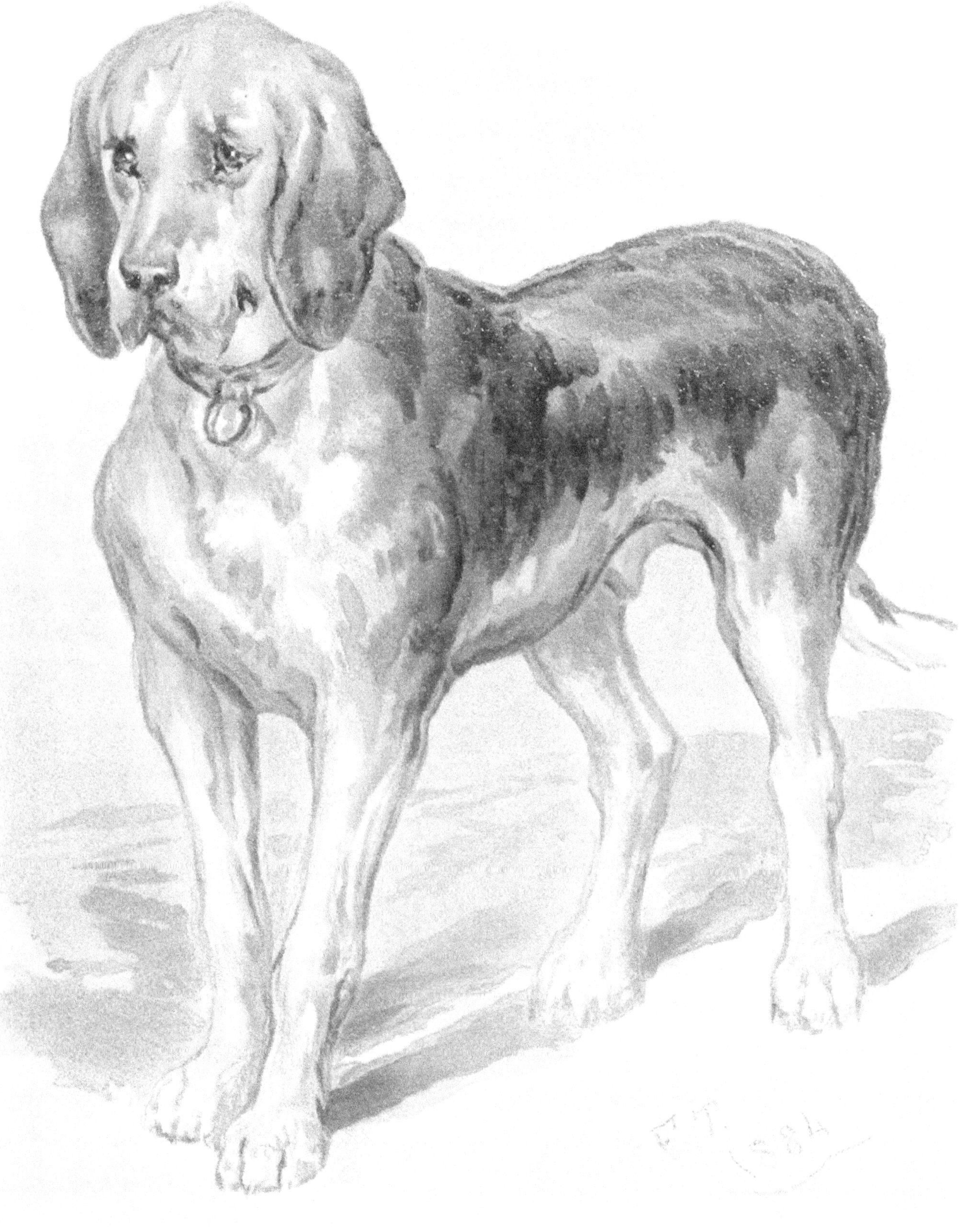

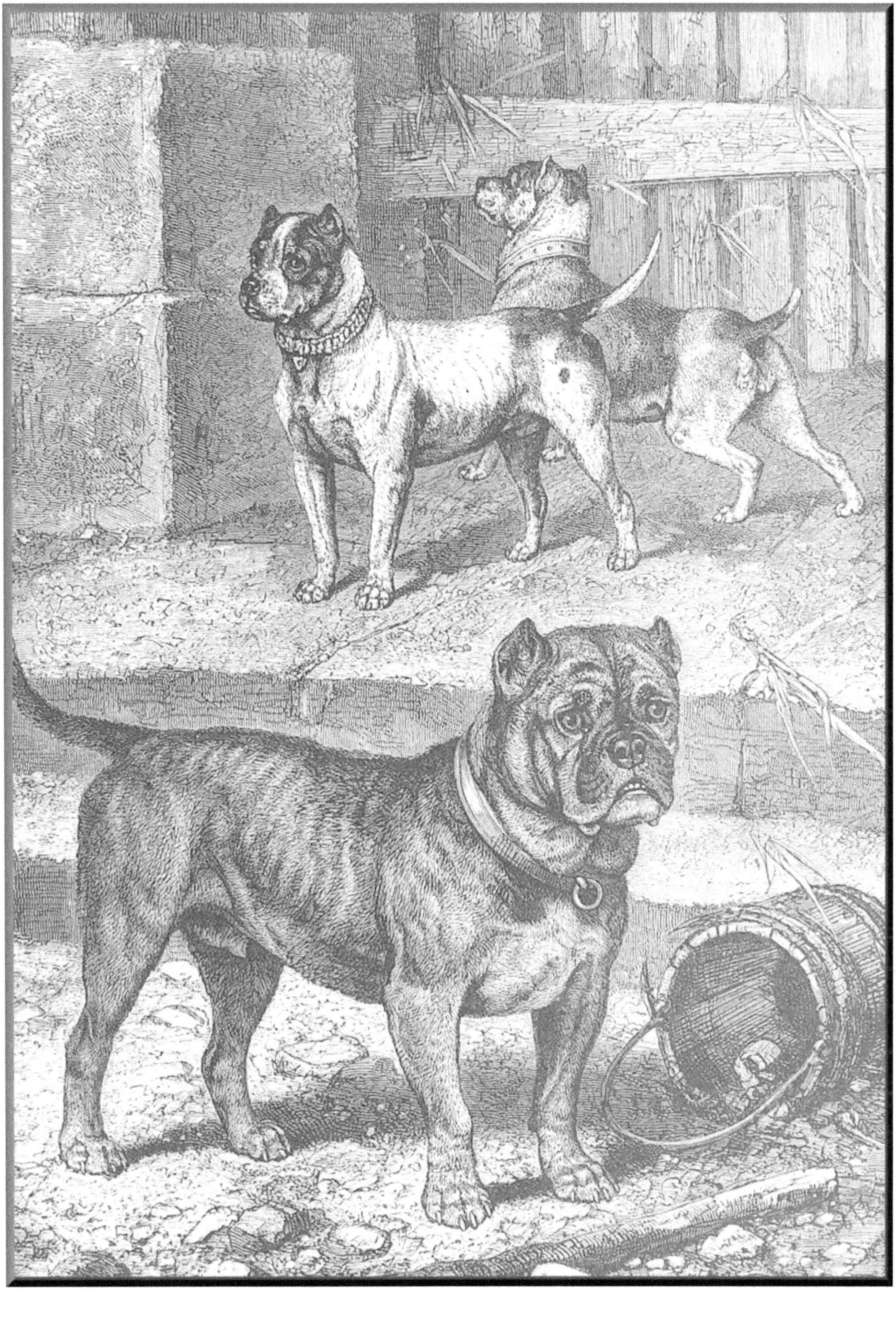

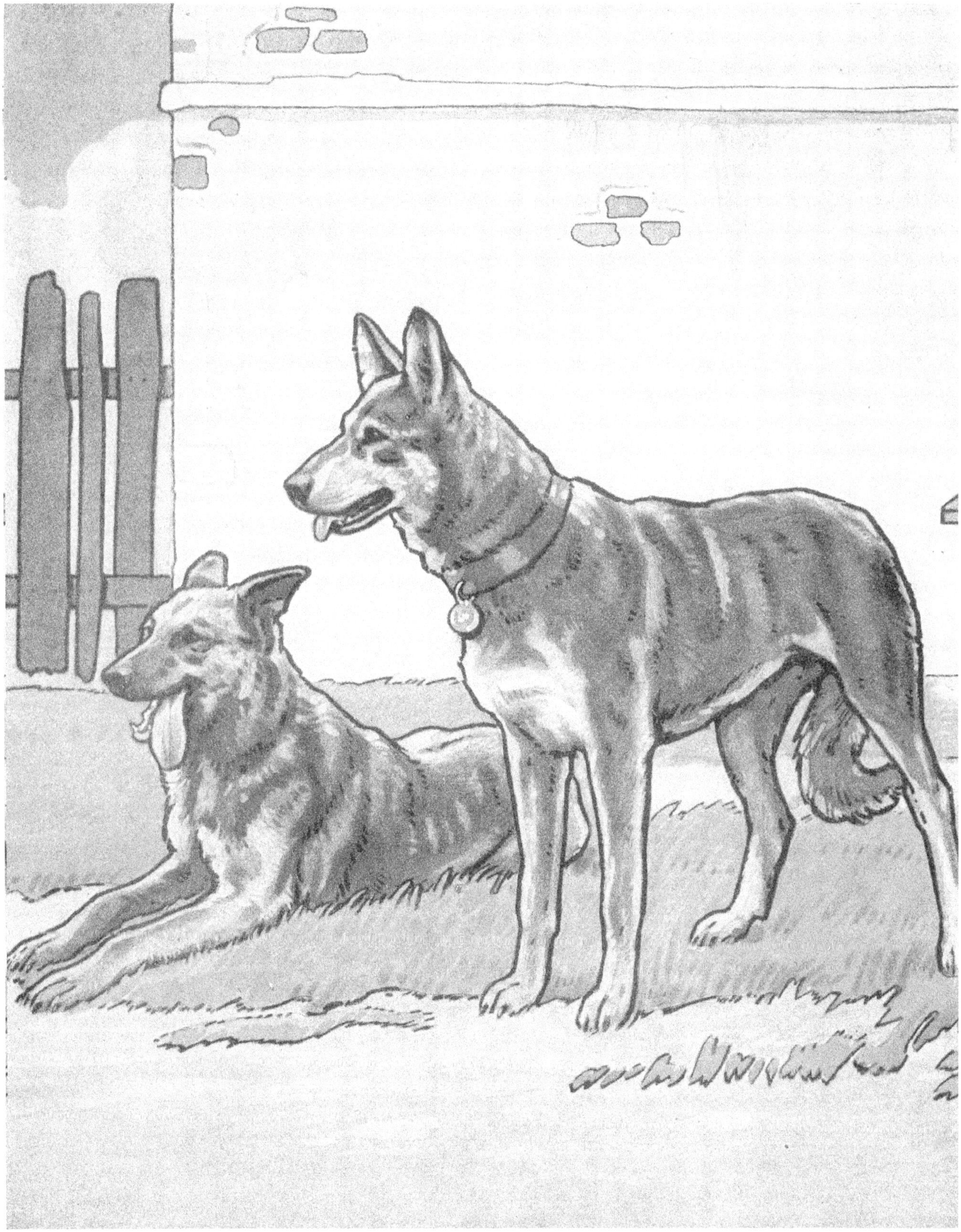

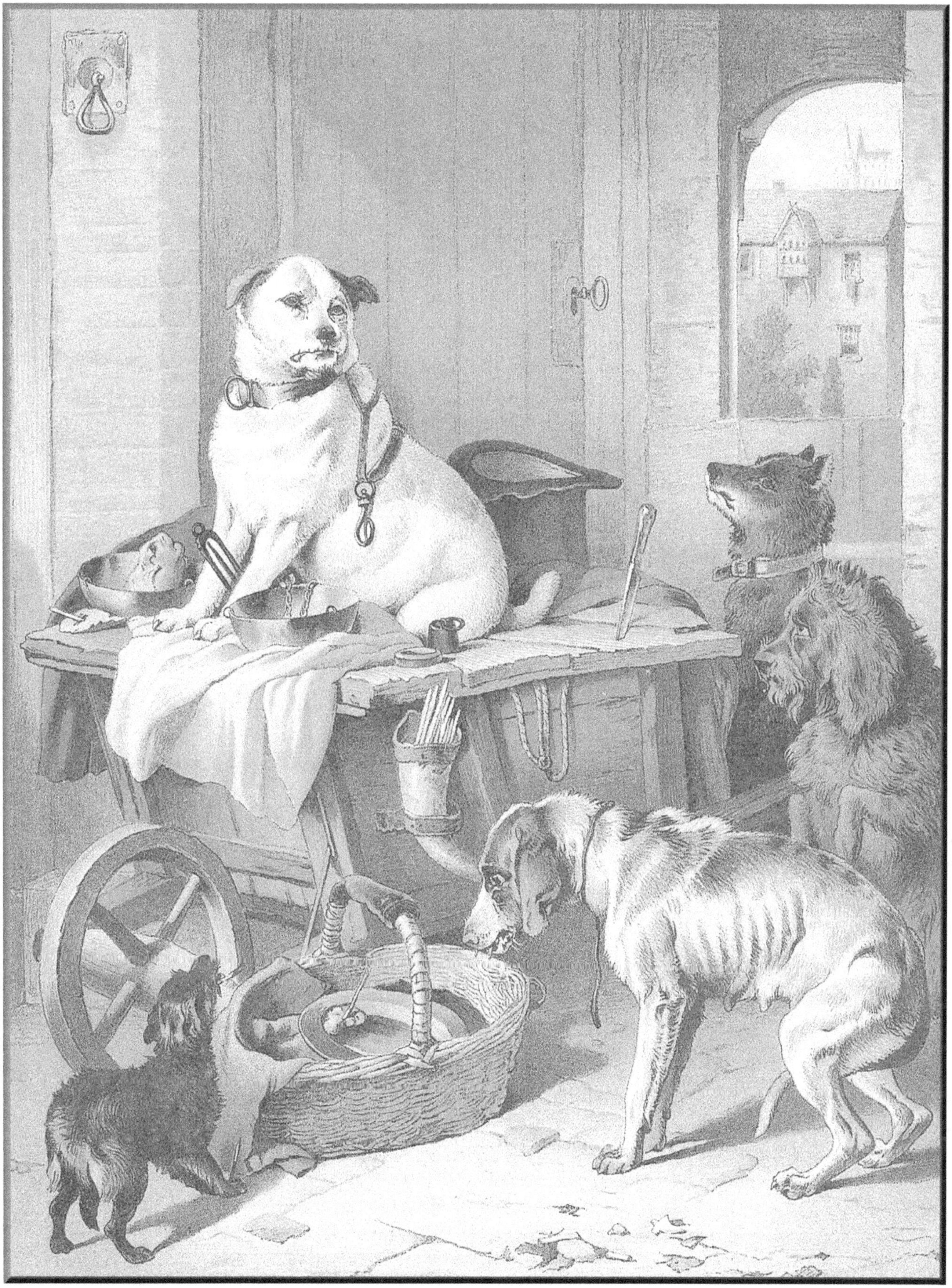

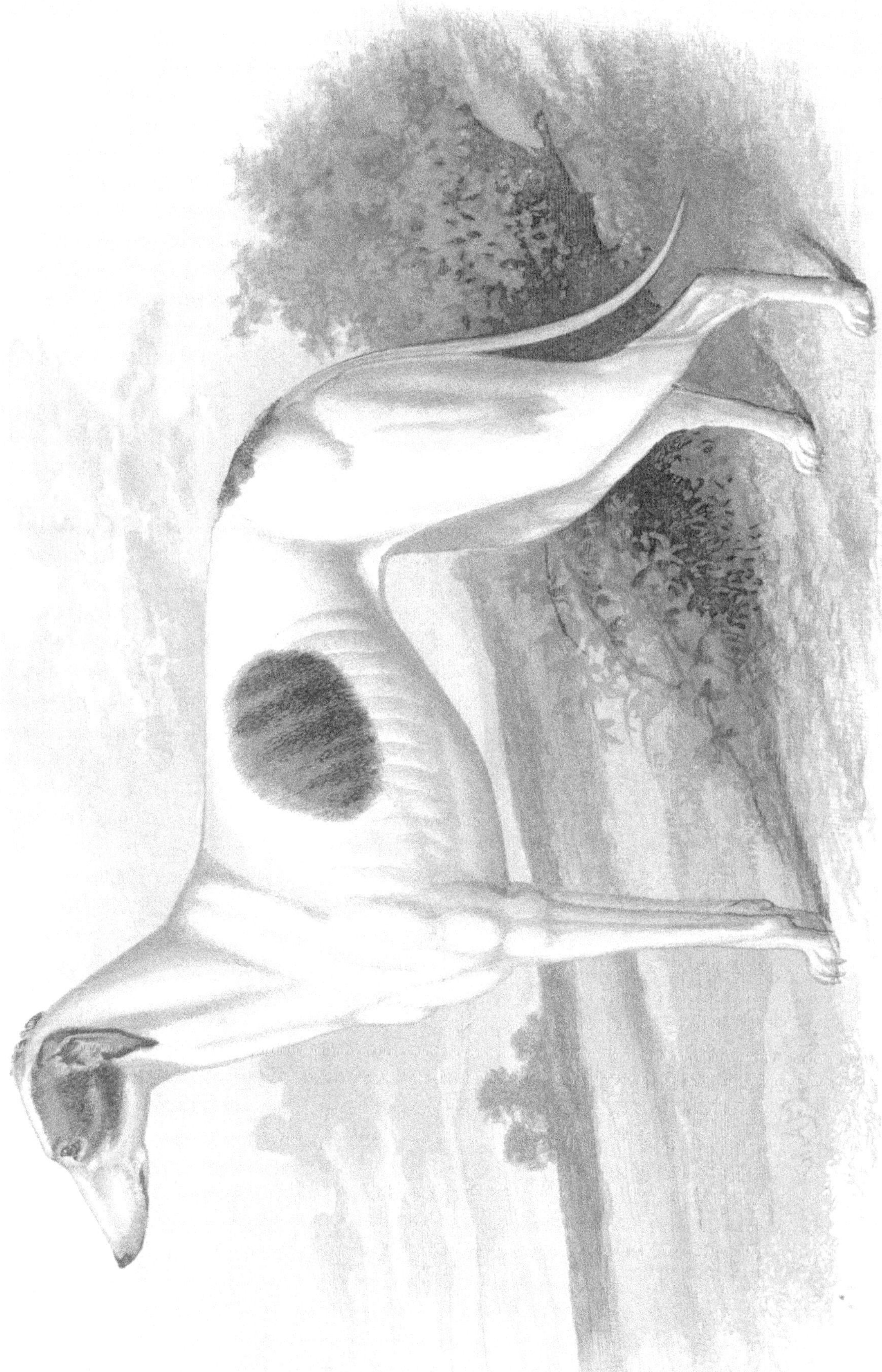

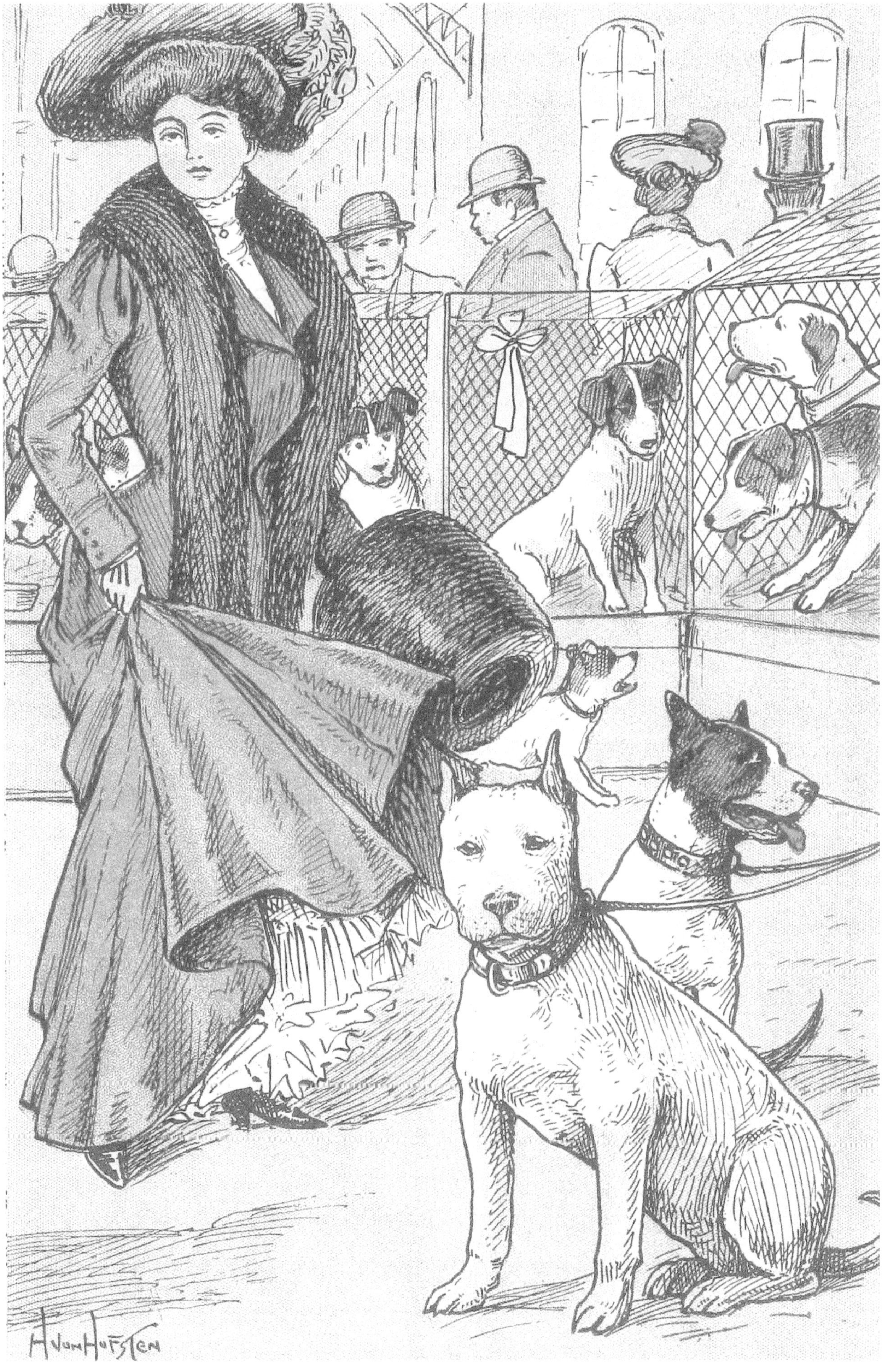

H VON HOFSTEN

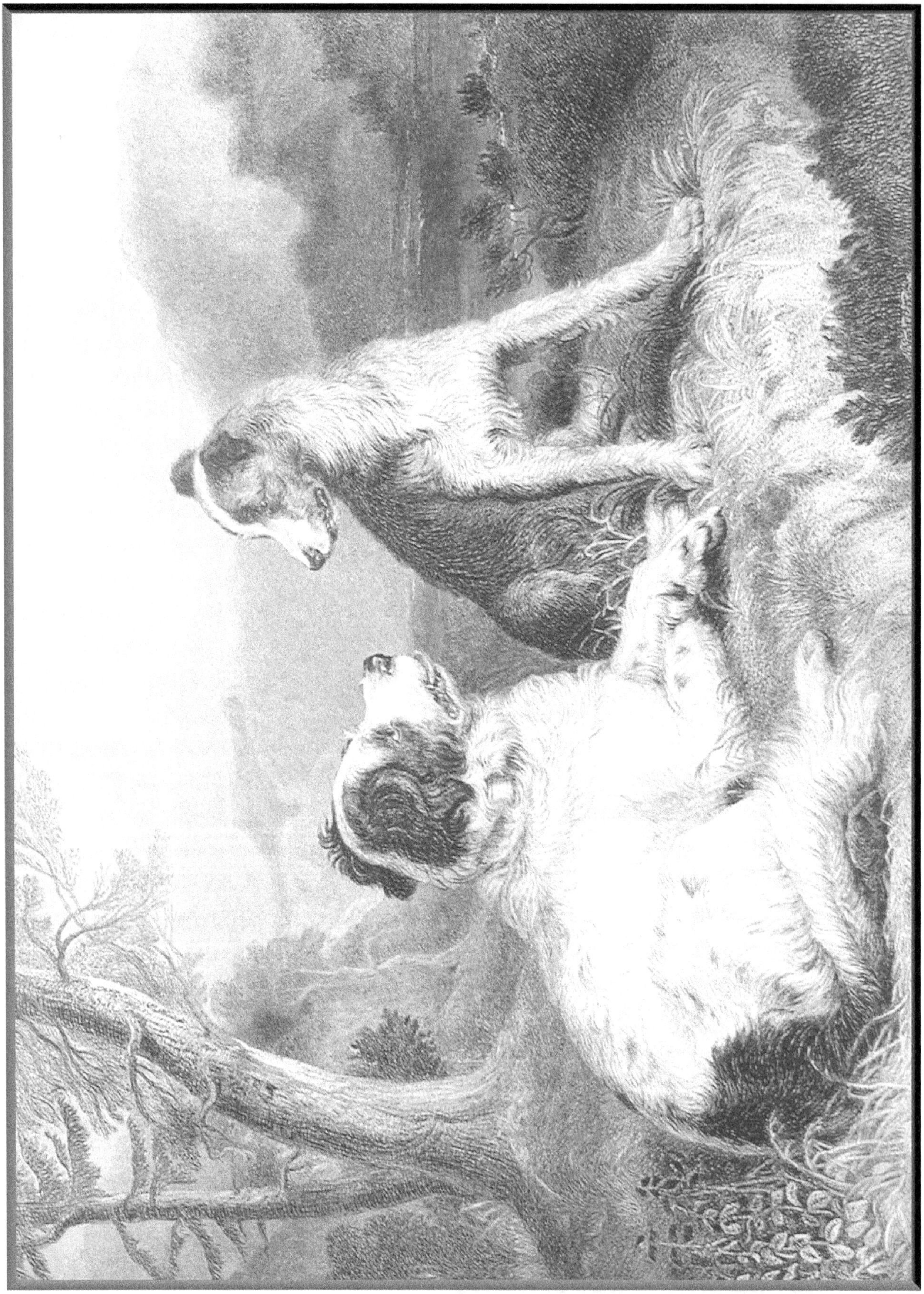

www.ingramcontent.com/pod-product-compliance
Lightning Source LLC
Chambersburg PA
CBHW080702190526
45169CB00006B/2204
* 9 7 8 1 5 3 4 9 8 6 8 2 4 *